gardenwatch

gardenwatch

Sarah Whittley

NEW HOLLAND

First published in 2008 by
New Holland Publishers (UK) Ltd
London • Cape Town • Sydney • Auckland

www.newhollandpublishers.com

Garfield House, 86–88 Edgware Road, London, W2 2EA,
United Kingdom
80 McKenzie Street, Cape Town, 8001, South Africa
Unit 1, 66 Gibbes Street, Chatswood, NSW 2067, Australia
218 Lake Road, Northcote, Auckland, New Zealand

Artwork by Cy Baker, Dan Cole, David Daly, Sandra Doyle/Wildlife
Art Ltd, Brin Edwards, Bridgette James and Dr Michael Roberts/The
Art Agency

ISBN 978 1 84773 112 8

Although the publishers have made every effort to ensure that
information contained in this book was meticulously researched and
correct at the time of going to press, they accept no responsibility for
any inaccuracies, loss, injury or inconvenience sustained by any
person using this book as reference.

Publishing Director: Rosemary Wilkinson
Commissioning Editor: Simon Papps
Editor: Liz Dittner
Photography: Howard Bottrell (www.ecovisuals.com)
Design: Sue Rose (Casebourne Rose Design Associates)
Production: Melanie Dowland

Reproduction by Modern Age Repro House Ltd, Hong Kong
Printed and bound in Singapore by Craft Print International

10 9 8 7 6 5 4 3 2 1

contents

PART ONE

ABOVE from left: Common Lizard, Blackcap, cranefly.
PAGE 3: the female wolf spider protects her eggs in a sac that is attached
to her spinnerets so that she is free to hunt.

PART TWO

INTRODUCTION

For many of us a garden is a place to relax, unwind and generally enjoy the outdoors while essentially remaining within the safety of our homes. However, gardens are an increasingly important habitat for an incredible variety of British wildlife, and in some cases they can play a vital role in the continued survival of healthy populations of certain species. While we are sitting sipping our drinks or sunning ourselves, the never-ending quest for survival is unfolding right before our very eyes.

There are in excess of 15 million gardens in Britain, which collectively cover more ground than any single national park in the country. The aim of this book is to highlight the wildlife potential of your garden and to enable you to track down which species are actually using it. You can then develop your interest further by contributing observations to national surveys and schemes which monitor garden wildlife.

In Part One of the book you will find information on how to encourage wildlife, how best to look after it and what equipment you might need. The second part is a seasonal guide to the wildlife you might encounter in your garden. Scattered throughout the book are ideas which may prompt you to become a 'Citizen Scientist' and join the army of wildlife-watchers who enjoy finding out more about the creatures with which they share their garden.

RIGHT: if space is available, leaving a wild patch in the garden is a great way to attract a wide range of species.

The garden habitat

It **is clear** that gardens are an increasingly important habitat for wildlife in Britain. This may sound strange when you consider our many wonderful native habitats such as coast, forest, farmland, freshwater, grassland and mountains. Can gardens really be included as a viable and sustainable habitat for wildlife? Considering the number of species that visit gardens throughout the year and rely on them for food and shelter, you have to take them very seriously, especially when you consider that there are more than one million acres of private gardens in Britain. Over the years, many of our natural wildlife habitats have been decreasing, whether it is through hedgerow and woodland destruction, marsh drainage or general countryside development, which is why many creatures now turn to gardens for refuge.

Hopefully this situation will change and the future is looking more promising with the introduction of many incentives for farmers and landowners to look after their land in a more wildlife-friendly way, the Environmental Stewardship Scheme being one example.

In fact, the habitat in gardens is not all that different from woodland or farmland. Although we tend to think of these as being 'natural' habitats, they are really just highly managed components of the wider countryside. Just like gardens, they have inputs (fertilisers and pesticides in farmland for example) and outputs (both crops and timber are harvested). So, while a garden may be highly managed, that does not make it any different from most other habitats. The birds, animals and insects that use the garden habitat will view it as a series of resources (feeding, breeding and sheltering opportunities) just as they do farmland and woodland and, in this way, it is as important as a piece of coppice or pasture.

The importance of the garden habitat has increased over time. To get some idea as to just how important it has become it is worth looking at a few facts and figures about other British habitats. During the past 50 years 75 per cent of ponds have been lost, three-quarters of Britain's butterfly species have decreased in numbers, two-thirds of Britain's woodland butterfly species have been classified as threatened, 10 per cent of British dragonfly species have become extinct and 25 per cent of bird species are declining. Since the Second World War, 97 per cent of our wildflower meadows have been destroyed, more than 200,000

LEFT: garden ponds provide valuable breeding habitat for dragonfly species such as Southern Hawker.

RIGHT: the Comma butterfly gets its name from the small white comma shape on each underwing. It is one of the few butterfly species to have increased in Britain in the past 50 years and its liking of gardens has no doubt helped.

ABOVE: Greenfinches love seed and peanut feeders. It is one of the 10 most commonly recorded birds in the BTO's Garden BirdWatch survey.

despondent, look at the figures regarding the garden habitat. Consider that there are more than 500,000 hectares of gardens in the UK – that is equivalent to 3 per cent of the total land area. If everyone gardened with wildlife in mind, already you can see the potential. Collectively, gardens form important wildlife corridors and in London alone about one-fifth of the total area is covered with gardens.

Wildlife is very adaptable. More than 60 species of birds have been recorded using nestboxes, while other birds, such as those that are suffering from the effects of habitat loss within farmland, are visiting gardens to feed during the difficult late winter period on a more regular basis, for example, Reed Bunting, Yellowhammer and Bullfinch. By feeding the birds we have helped many species, including Blue and Great Tits, Dunnock and Blackbird, not to mention Greenfinch, Goldfinch and Great Spotted Woodpecker. The Common Frog is a garden wildlife success story. Up until the 1970s its numbers were declining but now, with so many people installing wildlife ponds, numbers appear to be relatively stable. Thirty of Britain's 64 species of land mammals have been recorded visiting gardens.

miles of hedgerows have been removed and half of our ancient woodlands and three-quarters of our heaths have disappeared. A staggering 98 per cent of our lowland raised bogs have been destroyed, largely due to gardeners' insatiable appetite for using peat. About 150 species have become extinct in Britain due to habitat loss in the last 100 years. Twenty-two species of wildflowers have gone and a further 317 are at risk. With the introduction of genetically engineered crops we run the risk of losing yet more of our countryside's biodiversity, and this could potentially be devastating for our wildlife.

There is little cause for cheer after reading these statistics but, just in case you are beginning to feel

ABOVE: gardens provide a refuge where many wild plant species such as Ramsons can flourish.

ABOVE: the shy and elusive Bullfinch is more at home in hedgerows, but gardens with fruit trees will certainly appeal to this species, which is fond of buds.

The importance of gardens

ABOVE: it is a good idea to keep a pad and pen on the windowsill so you can note down date and time of day of sightings.

Once you have established what species you have in your garden, or at least become more in tune with the rhythm of your garden's natural history, you will probably want to start writing down your sightings. Recording wildlife sightings for your own pleasure can be as straightforward as recording daily notes in a blank book or page-a-day diary or sharing sightings and photos with like-minded people via websites – some of the most popular are *Over the Garden Gate* (www.gardenchat.com), *Wild About Britain* (www.wildaboutbritain.co.uk) and *UK Safari* (www.uksafari.com).

For some people, though, the more scientific approach is preferable, especially if you want to make comparisons over the years. It is important to collate your observations in a systematic way and you can do this by participating in some of the national surveys listed below. Alternatively, you can buy software that is specifically designed for collecting such data – two companies that produce such packages are Mapmate (www.mapmate.co.uk) and Wildlife Computing Ltd (www.wildlife.co.uk).

If you would like to participate in wildlife recording surveys and schemes around the country, there are many organisations that can help. There are a number of schemes that require you to venture no further than your living room or kitchen window. For birds, the British Trust for Ornithology (www.bto.org) and the RSPB (www.rspb.org.uk) run many schemes. The Mammal Trust (www.mtuk.org) and The Mammal Society (www.abdn.ac.uk/mammal) perform a similar function for mammals, as do Buglife (www.buglife.org.uk) for insects and Plantlife (www.plantlife.org.uk) for plants.

Submitting records to organisations such as these really does make a difference. Over a long period of time enough information can be collated to determine trends that could be vital for the survival of species in a regional or even a national context. Such databases can also be instrumental in helping us to achieve a greater understanding of the behaviour and habitat requirements of all kinds of species. So why not become a citizen scientist? Record and send in your garden sightings and you really will be making a difference.

For a more detailed list of current surveys, see the 'Useful websites' section towards the end of this book.

ABOVE: Early Bumblebee. You can make a serious and useful contribution to bumblebee survival by submitting your sightings to www.bumblebeeconservationtrust.co.uk.

Getting involved in survey work

Have you ever read an amazing fact in a field guide and thought 'How do they know that?' Most of the time we can thank the diligence of scientists and researchers. However, there are now several schemes run by various organisations that enable anyone to become an indispensable citizen scientist. Survey work plays a vital role in the conservation of many species; if more people get involved, we will be gaining important information not only on conservation status, but animal behaviour and trends. It is also very satisfying to know that while you are enjoying yourself watching wildlife, you could also be contributing towards the survival of many species.

Bird surveys

The British Trust for Ornithology (BTO) and The Royal Society for the Protection of Birds (RSPB) both run national surveys through which you can get involved in recording the birds in your garden. This is important information that can help to illustrate population changes over time.

The RSPB's annual Big Garden Birdwatch

ABOVE: among the many theories as to the House Sparrow's dramatic decline in towns are the removal of hedges and bushes and the covering of many gardens with decking and paving. The yellow gape helps to identify this bird as a fledgling.

(www.rspb.org.uk/birdwatch) is the world's biggest bird survey. Anyone can take part and all you need is an hour's spare time once a year in January. On a fixed weekend more than 400,000 people in more than 200,000 gardens will be counting their gardens' birds for this survey. The information gathered helps the RSPB to understand bird populations and which species are increasing or decreasing. The 2007 survey showed an overall decrease in bird numbers, although this might have been due to the mild winter, where birds did not need to come in search of extra food. The 2007 survey showed the House Sparrow is the most common species, followed by the Starling; a result that is somewhat ironic as House Sparrow numbers were calculated to have fallen by 56 per cent since 1979 and Starling numbers by a massive 76 per cent over the same period.

The BTO's Garden BirdWatch (www.bto.org/gbw/) encourages people to note down their bird sightings during the course of each week. The information can then be submitted weekly over the internet or by special forms that cover a 13-week period, which can be posted. More than 16,500 people around the country already record their birds in this way. Once all the information is received, it is added to the national Garden Birdwatch database. This helps to make up a pattern, which can help the BTO to determine trends, behaviour and populations. The BTO will be alerted if, for example, there is a sudden influx of certain species or, more importantly, a sudden decline.

Other bird recording schemes that are relevant to garden birdwatchers include the BTO's BirdTrack, nest record and ringing schemes. BirdTrack (www.bto.org/birdtrack/), which evolved from the BTO's Migration Watch survey, is a year-round bird-recording scheme which is designed to collect large numbers of bird sightings. The focus is on spring and autumn migration, seasonal movements and the distribution of scarce species. BirdTrack sightings can be posted on the internet (www.bto.org/birdtrack/), while results are also made available there. The BTO's Nest Record Scheme (see www.bto.org/survey/nest_records/) has been running since 1939 and data collected has enabled the trust to investigate changes in breeding success over time. Participants can submit records for any species in any habitat, including gardens. Birds are ringed to record their movements, calculate their chances of survival and monitor their population health. Anyone can contribute to these studies by reporting any ringed birds using the online reporting form (www.bto.org/ringing/ringinfo). The BTO will reply with details of when and where 'your' bird was ringed.

Mammal surveys

The Mammal Trust (www.mtuk.org) currently runs a Living with Mammals survey where the public can make a marked difference by submitting sightings. Its aim is to determine how our mammals use the built environment and the green spaces within it and it requests all mammal sightings from your chosen study area, whether it is a garden or a park.

The trust also has a Mammals on Roads survey that relies on people submitting sightings of wild road-kill mammals in order to gain information on the distribution and populations in the wider countryside. The Mammal Trust has already estimated that 100,000 Foxes and 100,000 Hedgehogs are killed annually by cars, along with 50,000 Badgers and 50,000 deer. Counting road-kill allows conservation and management efforts to be targeted appropriately.

Both surveys rely on accurate identification, so if you feel that you need to hone your skills The Mammal Society (www.abdn.ac.uk/mammal) and The Mammal Trust both run various courses to help, including how to use live traps and how to identify mammals.

As well as these national schemes, you can also get involved in a variety of more local surveys. Your local

ABOVE: snails that are common in British gardens include (from top to bottom) Common Snail, White-lipped Snail, Rounded Snail and Strawberry Snail.

Wildlife Trust (www.wildlifetrusts.org) is a good place to start; they should be able to advise you on current schemes in your area. Many local councils also run schemes to help you get involved in the conservation of local wildlife, and most have a wildlife department.

Reptile and amphibian surveys

Reptiles and amphibians are frequent garden visitors, especially if you have a garden pond. To get more involved with these species, get in touch with the National Amphibian and Reptile Recording Scheme (NARRS – www.narrs.org.uk). This is a partnership project led by the Herpetological Conservation Trust (HCT) that aims to monitor the conservation status of all the country's amphibian and reptile species. They run many surveys including a Garden Amphibian Survey and a Garden Reptile Survey.

The Amphibian and Reptile Group (ARG-UK) is a network of wildlife volunteer groups which work closely with NARRS and aim to protect and conserve the native amphibians and reptiles of the UK. It is keen for people to send in any sightings of reptiles and amphibians from gardens (www.arg-uk.org.uk), while there is a useful identification guide on its website.

Insect surveys

Invertebrates are an essential component of a garden's (or indeed any habitat's) wildlife make-up. Among their many benefits are their role in pollinating plants, providing a food source for birds and animals and maintaining the soil in a healthy state – the list goes on and on. With such drastic changes in our countryside, genetically modified crops being just one example, monitoring the status of our insect life can play a vital role in ensuring our countryside's biodiversity. They are also a fascinating group to study with many beautiful species.

If you want to get involved in insect and bug surveys, the best place to start is the Invertebrate

ABOVE: one of the great things about watching moths is that they can be seen at any time of the year. The species shown here are all active during the day. They are (clockwise from top left): Jersey Tiger, Magpie, Angle Shades and Cinnabar.

Conservation Trust or Buglife (www.buglife.org), whose ongoing surveys include bumblebees, Glow-worms and National Moth Night .

If butterflies are your passion, you can start recording your sightings for the UK Butterfly Monitoring Scheme (www.ukbms.org). This commitment should not be undertaken lightly as you will need to survey your patch regularly, submit weekly recording forms and carry on the survey for at least five consecutive years. If you are interested, contact a regional co-ordinator via the UKBMS website, who will help you to set up a site or transect.

Encouraging wildlife into the garden

The best way to encourage wildlife into your garden is by providing a wealth of options in terms of food and shelter – by effectively making it the equivalent of the best five-star hotel in town. You will need to create as many different habitats as possible, include a good selection of suitable plants, supply plenty of food and water, erect specially made homes where natural ones are lacking and minimise any potential risks or hazards. For example, it is known that cats may kill various types of wildlife; if you have a cat that hunts, try attaching two small bells to its collar and keeping it in overnight – dawn is when most predation takes place. Research shows that cats can still hunt effectively with one bell by learning to move without making it ring, but with two bells they cannot move silently.

Leaving loose piles of leaves, grass clippings or straw creates ideal areas for a multitude of mini-beasts and small mammals. Similarly, log piles left in quiet areas of the garden act as a magnet for many creatures, including mice, Hedgehogs, invertebrates and Wrens. Instead of taking your garden clippings to the dump, leave them in a quiet corner of the garden until they break down naturally. If you decide to burn these piles, first ensure that a Hedgehog or some other animal has not taken up residence. Leaving seed-heads on perennials in autumn not only offers valuable food for birds and hibernation sites for insects, but they can continue to look very attractive through the winter, especially with a covering of frost. Two of the least wildlife-friendly actions that you can take in the garden are to put down vast areas of decking or paving stones, as both offer very little in terms of wildlife habitat.

LEFT: the Swallow is regular summer visitor to many gardens in the countryside. This species can be distinguished from the closely related House Martin by its dark throat and long tail streamers.

Birds

Keeping birdfeeders filled year-round will encourage resident birds to stay as well as enticing winter visitors and, if you are lucky, the odd passing migrant. Providing food in summer offers a helpful top-up for birds during the breeding season and can help them through their annual moult at the end of summer. This act of kindness can be expensive, though, so making the most of kitchen scraps and packets of lard and suet will help.

The main thing to remember regarding bird food is not to put out anything containing salt as the birds cannot tolerate it. White breadcrumbs are okay as a filler but they have hardly any nutritional value. If you want to use rice (preferably brown) make sure it is cooked and not raw, or it will swell in the birds' stomachs. Pastry and fruit will also be welcome.

During the breeding season cat food is a good, highly nutritional meal and is often sought after by Blackbirds. Having said this, there is no substitute for providing good quality food in the form of sunflower hearts or seed mixes. There are masses to choose from as any trip to a specialist bird food shop will confirm. The best thing to do is try out a few different types of seed and see what your birds like. Do not be fooled by cheap food because, invariably, it will be filled with inferior quality bulk food such as biscuits and grain.

Remember that different species of birds have different feeding preferences, so a range of foods is needed if you want to attract a variety of bird species. Try to support a local farmer if they are selling seed from their land. Birds such as thrushes and Blackbirds will be attracted to windfall fruit, so try to leave as much as you can lying around. Of course, offering natural food is a great bonus and it is well worth growing berry-producing shrubs and plants with good seed-heads. Last, but by no means least, keep a constant supply of fresh water for drinking and bathing.

Open nestbox

Standard nestbox

Treecreeper box

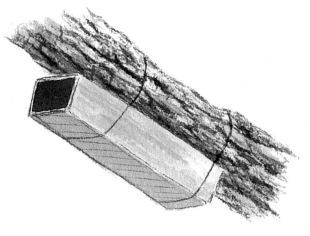

Owl box

Another important thing to remember is always to keep your feeding stations clean. Birds can carry a number of diseases and these can be passed from one bird to another where they gather together to feed. A weekly clean using one part of disinfectant (you can buy a toxic-free version) to 10 parts of water will keep your birdtable disease free. Make sure that you rinse and dry the items thoroughly. Droppings quickly accumulate in water containers, so rinse them out regularly, daily in warmer weather.

In many ways the garden habitat mimics or replaces a woodland or woodland edge habitat. In the wild, many birds make their nests in natural nooks and crannies in trees; simulating these sites is surprisingly easy with the help of nestboxes. Not only will they help the birds, but they will also offer great viewing opportunities to you throughout the breeding months. Various types of nestbox are commonly used in gardens. The standard box has a circular entrance hole

tracks or strands of fur stuck to fences, half-eaten remnants of food, or a lawn scattered with holes or faeces. However, with a little detective work you can usually find out which species have been visiting. One of the best methods is by track identification – finding tracks is easy with snow on the ground; failing that try making a muddy area around a feeding station. Another is to look for signs of feeding or faeces which could be identified. If this proves too difficult, some people find that setting live traps can be very helpful,

ABOVE: to minimize the risk of disease, remember to clean your bird-table every week. Use boiling water, one part bleach to 10 parts water.

in the front – the size of the box and the hole vary for different species and they can be built so that they are suitable for tits, sparrows, Common Redstarts or Starlings. The open box is similar to the standard but with the top half of the front cut away. This can attract Robins, Pied Wagtails and Spotted Flycatchers. Slightly more specialised boxes include the Treecreeper box – a wedge-shaped box with a hole in the top of the side – and the much larger, rectangular owl box for Tawny Owls.

It is essential to clean out nestboxes each year but, because nesting birds are protected by law, this should only be done between 1 August and 31 January. Nestboxes are sometimes used by roosting birds during the winter. You can also buy or make special roosting pockets which can be placed around the garden to help birds such as Wrens to survive freezing weather. These are usually made from natural fibres and protected with a wooden top.

Mammals

Encouraging mammals into the garden is not necessarily very difficult, but actually getting good views of them or even spotting them in the first place can be incredibly tricky. At best you may find their

ABOVE: nestboxes can be used during winter as communal roost sites for birds such as Wrens, which huddle together for warmth during the coldest nights.

ABOVE: bats are communal creatures, so if possible try to erect more than one bat box, and place them next to each other in the garden.

gadgetry, try adopting a more technical approach such as night photography with infrared, timers or movement triggers, all of which can be can very useful.

As with many humans, the way to an animal's heart is through its stomach, so leaving tasty morsels out on a regular basis is a good way to encourage garden visits. Try to vary the foods provided as much as possible so as not to make the animal too dependent. For small mammal watching, build a table on the ground with mesh over the top to deter cats or Foxes. Put out a general bird seed mix, peanuts and fruit for most rodents. Alternatively you can make something far more grandiose, by building a framework with very fine mesh (less than 1 cm) around a table in front of a window. Make some holes no larger than 3-4 cm in diameter (to stop rats getting in) and sit back and wait.

but this should not be undertaken lightly. If you are very keen and do not mind investing in the latest

By installing bat boxes in your property, not only might you be helping to save a vulnerable species – six

getting involved
MAKE A HEDGEHOG BOX

To make the simplest of Hedgehog homes, all you need is a box. If it is wooden make sure that it has not been treated with any preservative. You can also use heavy-duty cardboard boxes; banana boxes are great as they have slide-down lids that make them very sturdy. Once you have a box, cut an entrance hole of about 10 cm in diameter. Make the box waterproof by covering it with a plastic sheet – split plastic bags will do – then heap over piles of garden waste such as twigs, leaves and cut grass. You can improve this basic model by making your own wooden box (30 cm high x 40 cm wide) and adding an entrance tunnel about 60 cm long and 10 cm

high. Do not make the entrance much bigger than that as cats and foxes could be tempted to come in and take a sleeping Hedgehog as prey. A ventilation pipe, with chicken wire wrapped around the ends to stop leaves from blocking it, can also be added.

Providing food or shelter can encourage Hedgehogs into gardens.

British species are endangered – but you will be increasing your chances of observing individuals of the world's only true-flying mammal family. At least 13 of Britain's 17 bat species have roosted in bat boxes and Brown Long-eared, Daubenton's, Noctule, Leisler's, Natterer's and Common and Soprano Pipistrelles have actually used them for breeding. Bats need boxes in the summer for rearing young and roosting and in the winter for hibernation. Summer boxes need to be large enough for multiple use. Most are made of wood but cement boxes also work very well. Winter boxes come in two forms, one for outdoors and the other for use indoors in cellars and tunnels. Bricks with multiple hollow chambers (bat bricks) can also be used when constructing or replacing existing brickwork.

Although you can buy bat boxes in specialist stores, making your own is also an option. Take a plank of wood 150 mm by 1,100 mm. The back plate is 330 mm, the front 140 mm, the base 90 mm (with an entrance slit of 15-20 mm) and the roof 200 mm. Sides are 200 mm at their highest, sloping to 140 mm at their lowest, There are many websites with excellent instructions for building your own box, such as the Norfolk Bat Group's (www.norfolk-bat-group.org.uk) and the Lincolnshire Wildlife Trust's (www.lincstrust.org.uk).

Bat boxes can be attached to either a building or a tree, but it is best to put about three boxes together and always remember to place them as high up as possible to avoid predators. Winter boxes need to be put up in a cool, shaded place as waking up during a warm blast of winter sunshine can be very damaging for the bats. The Bat Conservation Trust website (www.bats.org.uk) is a good source of information about British bats.

The best way to see Hedgehogs is to feed them; cat or dog food, including small cat biscuits, chopped peanuts, sultanas or raisins, mealworms and special Hedgehog mix should supplement their diet. Beetles and caterpillars are their preferred food but they will also eat birds' eggs, slugs, snails, carrion and even small rodents' young if pushed. In fact, they will eat pretty much anything!

You can help Hedgehogs in winter by providing suitable areas in your garden for hibernation. Piles of leaf litter, compost or brushwood are all suitable, although if you want to make sure that your Hedgehog hibernates in style, there are various artificial homes you can make or buy. You can buy Hedgehog boxes from many specialist stores – typical dimensions are about 30 cm wide by 50 cm long at the bottom and 25 cm high, although these can vary.

Invertebrates

As with birds and mammals, invertebrates will visit your garden if you offer them something to eat, somewhere to live, or both. There are a few simple things you can do if space allows, such as leaving areas for nettles and other native plants or letting part of

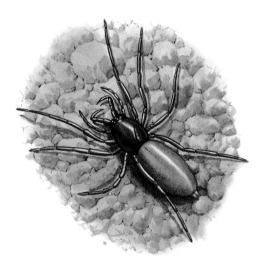

ABOVE: a pale, oval abdomen contrasting with a rusty body and legs help to identify the Woodlouse-eating Spider.

ABOVE: gardens host a range of fascinating insects including (clockwise from top left) Black-and-red Froghopper, Thick-legged Flower-beetle, Dock Bug and Cockchafer. The greater the number of native plant species in your garden, the more species will be attracted.

your lawn grow wild. Planting nectar- and pollen-rich plants which provide food throughout the year will encourage insects, especially bees, butterflies and moths.

Rotten logs and piles of wood are great year-round homes for a variety of invertebrates, especially beetles. Many species occur in gardens, and if you are very fortunate you may find the rare Stag and Lesser Stag Beetles. You may also find various millipedes, woodlice, centipedes and spiders. Keep an eye out for the Woodlouse-eating Spider – as the name suggests, it will often be found close to its favoured prey.

Many hibernating insects look for warm, wind-free nooks and crannies to crawl into before they shut

down. By simply drilling 90 mm holes into a block of wood and placing it in a sheltered part of the garden you will have created a ready-made home that is suitable for various insects, including solitary wasps, solitary bees, beetles and spiders. Alternatively you can use a piece of drainpipe and then pack it tightly with straws or bamboo canes, between 5-8 mm in diameter. Block one end off to stop draughts and hang it in a sheltered part of the garden.

Terracotta plant pots can make a good hibernation homes for the queens of certain species of bumblebee. There are various ways you can adapt the pots and it may be worthwhile experimenting to see which works

The Bumblebee Conservation Trust (www.bumblebeeconservationtrust.co.uk) is looking for volunteers to test different types of nestboxes because, even though they sell well, it can be difficult to get the bees to use them. Its website also has a useful guide to bee identification.

ABOVE: careful study of bumblebees will enable you to identify the various British species, many of which frequently occur in gardens.

for you. One method is to lay a large plant pot on its side and stuff with it with Kapok fibre and hay, then bury it, leaving a length of pipe from the drainage hole (2 cm in diameter) for entry. Or you can upend a smaller plant pot with the same stuffing, leaving the base just showing above the soil so the drainage hole is exposed. Bumblebee boxes are used by the colony during the breeding months; they are similar to bird boxes but are divided into two.

There are 46 species of ladybird in Britain, although only 26 are easily recognisable. All gardeners welcome our native species due to the voracious appetite for plant-harming aphids that is shared by both the adults and larvae. Encouraging them to hibernate through the winter will ensure a constant, chemical-free aphid destroyer. The only unwelcome species is the Harlequin Ladybird, which was introduced into America from south-east Asia as a form of pest control. It has the potential to devour many of our native ladybird species if other food is not available.

Specially made ladybird houses can be bought to simulate the insects' natural hibernation hideaways, which are in dark crevices such as behind tree bark

ABOVE: leaving a rotting log in the garden will seem like a five-star hotel for lots of wildlife, especially bugs, lichens and fungi.

and in hollow grass stems. To save money you can make your own, but remember that ladybirds often hibernate in large numbers, with sometimes as many as 1,000 gathering together. With this in mind make a large, open-ended birdbox with sloping, waterproof lid, partitioned with several pieces of wood about 1 cm apart.

Lacewings are another invaluable gardener-friendly species whose larvae eat vast quantities of aphids. Instead of buying a home you can make one out of a large plastic drink bottle filled with corrugated cardboard. Cut off the bottom of the bottle, making sure the plastic overhangs by about 5 cm, secure the cardboard with some wire and hang it in a sheltered spot in the garden.

Amphibians and reptiles

If you want to attract newts, frogs and toads to your garden, the best thing to do is install a pond. All of Britain's amphibian species visit ponds to breed in late winter or early spring. Building a rockery or simply constructing a pile of rocks, bricks or slabs in the garden, preferably near to the pond, will provide them with an ideal place to hibernate. In building your 'rockery', the aim is to create dark, cool chambers for the amphibians to crawl into. A quick and easy option is to dig a shallow hole with a sloping entrance and then place a paving slab on top.

Grass Snakes may be attracted to the pond as frogs make up a large part of their diet. They will also be interested in large piles of decaying leaves and compost heaps, which they use as nesting sites in late summer. By keeping an area of rough grass, a nesting site and a nearby pond you will be offering Grass Snakes their very own Shangri-La.

Finally, although they may not be the most attractive garden feature, sheets of corrugated metal provide great shelters for snakes, lizards, frogs and toads.

ABOVE: Common Lizards live in a wide range of habitats including heathland, woodland, sand dunes, hedgerows and gardens.

Garden wildlife-watching equipment

Binoculars

The most important piece of equipment for garden wildlife-watching is undoubtedly a good pair of binoculars. As you will use these more than anything else, try to spend as much on them as you can afford. Cheap binoculars can be a false economy and make wildlife-watching a misery; a good pair will bring the subject right up to you with crystal clarity and light, making the whole experience much more enjoyable. Try and get some advice from a specialist shop first and it is essential to try before you buy as different models suit different people. Remember that the RSPB has a great range of optics and if you buy from them you will be supporting a worthwhile cause.

When choosing binoculars think how often you will use them and where. Walking for miles with bulky, heavy binoculars can hurt, but the same pair might be okay if they are going to spend most of their life on the windowsill. If you like insect- or plant-watching, make sure you get binoculars that have close focusing – some focus down to less than 2 m.

Do not be fooled into thinking that bigger is better. A cheap, inferior pair of 10x40s will not be as good as a more expensive pair of 8x32s. Also, as the magnification increases, the brightness and clarity of the image usually diminish. To help explain the sizes, remember the first number indicates the magnification – which is usually from 7-10x – and the second number is the diameter of the objective lenses – which is usually from 20-50 mm. The most popular sizes for general birdwatching tend to be 8x30, 8x40 and 10x40.

Telescopes

Having a telescope set up on a tripod to watch the garden is more of a luxury than a necessity unless your garden is enormous. However, for longer-term observations, such as sketching from the scope or just watching in close-up, it can really make wildlife-watching a truly memorable experience.

Modern telescopes can have terrific magnification and produce a bright image while having compact and

Always spend as much as you can afford when buying binoculars; this is after all the most important piece of equipment for wildlife-watching.

lightweight bodies. Many now come with interchangeable eyepieces and most models have at least one zoom lens and a variety or fixed-focus wide-angle lenses available. It is worth trying both before you buy to see which you prefer, but remember that the wide-angle lens lets in more light and produces a brighter image that is particularly noticeable on dull days.

Attaching a camera to a telescope (a method of photography known as 'digiscoping') is good way of taking good close-up pictures without the extra expense of buying a powerful zoom lens. Seek advice from specialist stores before you buy anything and see the 'Useful addresses' section later in this book for helpful websites.

Cameras

A camera is a vital piece of equipment, especially if you want to share your experiences with other people. It is worth keeping a charged camera in the same place for quick access if needed.

A compact digital camera with a zoom is sufficient for most people, but if you find their confines too frustrating, buying an SLR (single reflex lens) camera is the thing to do. These cameras allow you to fix different lenses onto the body, so you can go from a macro close-focusing lens (for insects and plants) to a zoom lens for subjects far away or a wide-angle lens for landscapes. SLR photography is a complex subject and, if you are contemplating taking this more serious approach, you should seek professional help from at least two specialist shops before you buy anything, or chat to fellow wildlife photographers online through one of the websites mentioned at the end of the book.

Taking pictures at night can be tricky; flash photography can produce good results, but you will run the risk of terrifying your subject. Using a red filter over the flash can help with this.

ABOVE: using a tripod when photographing or digiscoping (as shown here) wildlife will reduce the risk of blurred pictures, especially in low light.

Video cameras and webcams

These days there is a vast array of technology and software that can be used for capturing images of garden wildlife; highly sophisticated spy technology is now being widely marketed for animal surveillance. Hand-held video cameras are great for shooting general garden wildlife; you can even attach some models to your telescope. Webcams and CCTV allow you to transfer live images directly to your website, computer or television. A sensor/infrared camera is able to take pictures automatically when triggered, which is ideal if you want to find out which beasts

ABOVE: getting good results from wildlife photography can be expensive; however, second-hand equipment is a great way to enjoy your hobby without burning too big a hole in your pocket.

keep raiding the flowerbed at night.

For the perfect peeping-tom experience, placing a miniature camera with a microphone in a nestbox can offer hours of televisual entertainment, although finding the right kit can be a daunting experience. The two types of technology commonly used are CMOS and CCD cameras. The latter produces better quality pictures but uses more power. For a better resolution look for a TVL (which stands for 'TV Lines') of greater than 380. Basically, cameras with a TVL of up to 380 are low to medium resolution and cameras with a TVL of greater than 380 have a higher resolution.

These cameras come in black and white or colour, although you will pay more for colour. If you have a black-and-white camera, infrared lights are the best way to illuminate your nestbox. For colour cameras it can be a little tricky; you can either choose a nestbox that lets in a certain amount of daylight or use an artificial white light bulb. You will need to turn these lights on and off, and the birds may find this annoying. Never put a camera in a box if the birds have already started nesting.

If you are going to start filming in nestboxes but are unsure about which equipment to use, please seek advice from one of the companies marketing these products, for example Ecowatch (www.eco-watch.com) who worked on the BBC's Springwatch series.

Hides

Using a hide is one of the best ways to observe and photograph wildlife unobtrusively and within very close range. Erecting a hide in front of a feeding station allows you to observe otherwise shy creatures, such as Jays and various rodents. If you have Yellow-necked Mice in your area you can get great views as they frequently raid birdtables.

You can buy specially made hides varying from the tiny, lightweight travelling type to the more substantial tent-like structures. If you do not have the funds, making your own hide is easily done. Try putting a length of tarpaulin over a wooden or tent-pole frame. A word of advice, though – leave enough space for a comfortable fold-up stool.

Magnifying lens

A magnifying lens is invaluable for watching botanical and invertebrate life. As with binoculars, the more you spend the better the quality. A pocket-sized hand-held

20 mm lens with 10x magnification will quickly become a favourite item.

Nets

If you want to catch insects, especially butterflies, moths and dragonflies, make sure you buy a specialist net with fine mesh so as not to harm their wings. It is best to have a separate net with less fine mesh to use for pond dipping.

Moth traps

There are a number of ways to attract moths, and perhaps the simplest is by setting up a 125W mercury vapour light bulb above a simple box with a narrow entrance where the insects can shelter. These can be bought or constructed and the *Atropos* website (www.atropos.info) has details of how to build your own and also how to encourage moths into your garden by using sugar solution or by putting in plants that are attractive to them.

ABOVE: moth-trapping is an exciting way to find out what species visit your garden. You can either buy traps or make your own.

ABOVE: in order to give the best results and to ensure that the subjects are not harmed, different types of net should be used for pond-dipping or insect-catching.

Live traps for small mammals

There are some golden rules to follow if you are going to use live traps. Most importantly, always remember to check your traps every three to four hours. Write down the locations where you place them and the times that you check them on a piece of paper and keep it somewhere obvious, and remember to set an alarm to go off every three or four hours when the traps are active. Traps should always be set with bedding, food and water.

Small mammal traps have two compartments, a tunnel which houses the door-tripping mechanism and a nestbox. You will know if you have caught something as the trapdoor will be shut. If this is the case, place the whole trap in a transparent plastic bag before you tip out the animal. Do not handle small mammals unnecessarily and always release them in exactly the same place that they were trapped. Lightweight, aluminum traps such as the Longworth are widely used although you can buy cheaper plastic alternatives, but remember that rodents can chew through plastic.

If you want to start trapping mammals contact The Mammal Society (www.abdn.ac.uk/mammal) for a copy of their booklet *Live Trapping Small Mammals: A Practical Guide* by John Gurnell and John Flowerdew. A licence is required if you are going to trap shrews, as these delicate mammals are protected by law.

Footprint tubes

These tubes are useful if you want to detect whether you have any mammal activity in your garden. The Mammal Society recommends that you make them by using an overflow pipe of 45 mm in diameter which has been cut to about 30 cm in length. Place a piece of paper within the pipe, with two lengths of greaseproof paper (7x4 cm) stapled just inside either entrance to act as 'inkpads'. Combine equal amounts of vegetable oil and poster paint and brush the mixture onto the greaseproof paper. As a lure, place a blob of peanut butter in the centre of the tube.

Torches

Any torch will be useful, but for serious night-time viewing in a large garden look at the high-powered torches that are available from specialist wildlife suppliers. These torches have either 500,000 candle power with 500 m spot beam or a massive 1,000,000 candle power with 1,000 m spot beam. These rechargeable torches allow you to attach a red filter to watch mammals unobtrusively. Simply putting a red filter over any torch will make the beam less obtrusive for wildlife.

Pooters

A pooter pot is a useful gadget for picking up insects without having to handle them. It has two tubes attached to a transparent pot; one tube you place over your subject and with the other you suck up quickly, forcing the insect into the pot.

Spiderdomes

Spiders can be very tricky to observe for any length of time, but you can attach a Spiderdome to a window, wall or tree and wait for your subject to climb in. The transparent dome has an opaque outer casing which can slide over when you are not viewing. In summer and autumn you might find spiders' eggs in the dome, while at other times of the year they will just visit for a short period.

ABOVE: attach some sort of red filter over the beam, so as not to blind your visiting nocturnal wildlife with a very powerful torch.

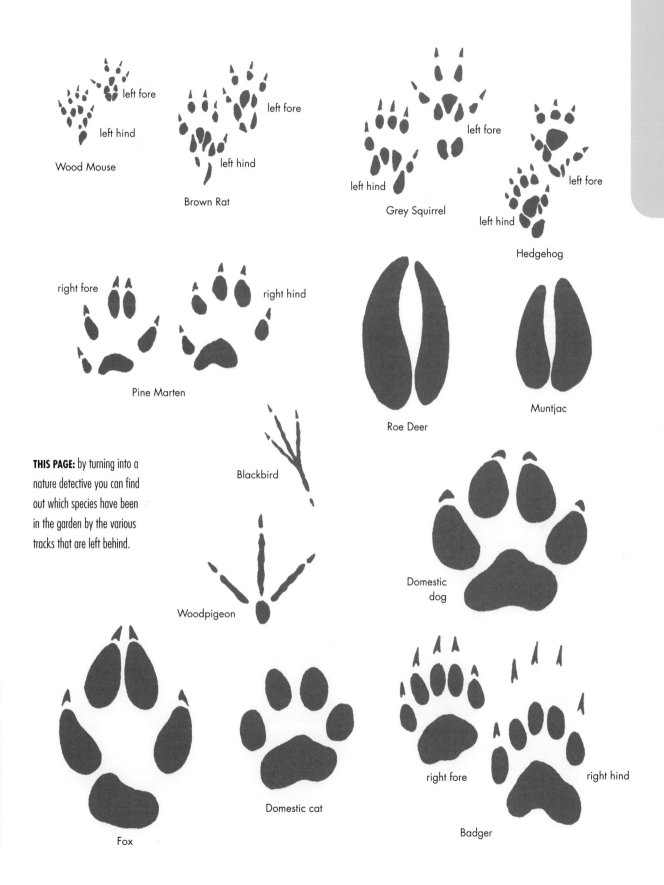

left fore

left hind

Wood Mouse

left fore

left hind

Brown Rat

left fore

left hind

Grey Squirrel

left fore

left hind

Hedgehog

right fore

right hind

Pine Marten

Roe Deer

Muntjac

THIS PAGE: by turning into a nature detective you can find out which species have been in the garden by the various tracks that are left behind.

Blackbird

Woodpigeon

Domestic dog

Fox

Domestic cat

right fore

right hind

Badger

WINTER
December to February

By December winter is truly upon us. All the autumn preparations made by garden wildlife will be tested over the next three months. Plants have shed their leaves, mammals have grown thick coats and feasted in preparation and sun-seeking birds have fled south to escape the onslaught of our coldest season.

There is little doubt that our winters are gradually becoming warmer; snow on Christmas Day is all but a distant memory for most people in Britain's lowlands. Prolonged snow showers are less common than they used to be and instead we are seeing more unseasonally warm, rainy, grey days.

Although our winters seem to be getting warmer, the unpredictability of our weather is always a threat. Just as we are relaxing in warm winter sunshine, the next day we can easily wake up to thick snow and freezing temperatures. And it is during these spells that wildlife needs our help.

LEFT: Roe Deer is one of the most likely deer species to visit gardens, especially in bad winter weather.

The garden

With little daylight time available for foraging, there is heightened activity amongst small mammals and birds in a desperate attempt to find enough food to stay alive. January brings with it the beginnings of new life; snowdrops and other hardy plants fight through the snow and frost and the slight increase in daylight hours triggers some animals into action. Squirrels start their courtship shenanigans and, if there is a prolonged warm spell, some birds, such as Robins and Blackbirds, are duped into nest-making and even egg-laying, although these very early attempts rarely reach fruition.

By February, which is traditionally our coldest month, there is much evidence of the eagerness of wildlife to break cover and shake off the winter torpor, especially on warm, sunny days. Some hibernating butterflies and bumblebees emerge, frogspawn suddenly appears and birds spring into amorous action.

Winter is probably the best time to spot some of the more elusive garden wildlife, especially during freezing weather. Birds and small mammals need to feed constantly to maintain fat levels, so that even the shyest of animals become uncharacteristically bold. Try putting out a feeding table for small mammals, with a banquet of fruit (including dried fruit), seeds and nuts, oats and other cereals, and you should see some activity. The most likely guests will be Field and Bank Voles, Wood and Yellow-necked Mice (the latter only occurs in southern England) and Hedgehogs.

If there has been overnight snowfall then get out first thing in the morning and look for tracks. This is an excellent way to find out which species live in your garden. Try to photograph or sketch the tracks before the snow melts.

Mammals

During winter, some animals that rely heavily on insects for food simply cannot find enough, and instead of enduring a precarious existence, they choose to hibernate. Only bats, Hedgehogs and dormice (including the native Common Dormouse and the introduced Edible Dormouse) hibernate in the UK. Other mammals such as squirrels and Badgers reduce their activity dramatically, sometimes choosing to sleep through very cold spells but always reappearing in warmer weather. Small mammals in particular need to work twice as hard to survive during these cold months. Throughout the winter, gardens are an important habitat for many visiting animals, although while some may choose to sleep, others will rely on us to keep them alive during the coldest weather.

December and January is a noisy time for Foxes as this is their mating season and if you have them living nearby you will certainly hear them. Females are often heard emitting a blood-curdling human-like scream around this time, which is probably to attract dog Foxes.

Hedgehogs must be among the most popular of all garden mammals and the sight of one trundling around your garden is hard to beat. Although they will take your offerings of food, these inquisitive insect-eaters are great for the garden as they will munch through piles of slugs, snails and caterpillars.

Around November, December or even as late as January, depending on the weather, Hedgehogs start to look for hibernation sites. Their nests, called hibernaculae, are frequently located in gardens. To say that an animal sleeps through winter is not quite accurate; in fact what hibernating animals do is pretty much shut down their bodies to the point of near death. The brain is almost inactive and the Hedgehog reduces its heartbeat from 190 beats per minute to just 20. They hardly draw breath and their body temperature drops from a normal 35°C to just 10°C. They should survive as long as their body temperature does not fall below 1°C.

ABOVE: the Wood Mouse is distinguished from the House Mouse by its larger eyes and ears and very long tail.

There are two very important things to remember when attracting Hedgehogs to your garden. Do not ever feed them milk, this can give them serious digestion problems resulting in diarrhoea. Secondly, always thoroughly check piles of garden waste before starting a bonfire as Hedgehogs and other creatures could have made this their home.

The best way to attract bats to your garden in winter is by offering them a comfortable hibernacula. Because bats eat flying insects, they are welcome garden guests, as a single pipistrelle can eat up to 3,000 insects per night. There are 17 species of bat in Britain, but the ones most likely to occur in the garden habitat are Common Pipistrelle, Soprano Pipistrelle and Brown Long-eared Bat. These bat species like to use our loft spaces or roof tiles for winter roosts, as well as cellars. Bat boxes are also readily used but do not be surprised if they fail to move in straight away; it can take years for bats to move into artificial homes and it often takes some sort of displacement nearby for it to happen.

Birds

Winter can be a cruel and unforgiving season for birds, particularly if it is a harsh one with prolonged freezing temperatures. Our gardens become crowded with extra birds, both residents and migrants, which have been driven there in a desperate attempt to find enough food to survive the long, cold nights. Species such as Robin and Blue Tit need to eat 30–40 per cent of their own body weight each day just to survive.

To add even more strain, birds fleeing the colder north European winter such as Fieldfares and Redwings, also visit our gardens. One of the most exotic-looking winter visitors that can turn up in

RIGHT: Fieldfares are particularly attracted to gardens during spells of hard weather and leaving apples on the lawn can help to draw them in.

ABOVE: studies have shown that April and June are the peak months for Goldfinches visiting gardens.

Keeping a simple weekly record of which birds you see in your garden can be very rewarding, especially if you submit these records to a national project like the British Trust for Ornithology's Garden BirdWatch scheme (www.bto.org/gbw). Some 16,000 people already do this, enabling researchers to understand how birds use gardens and how this use changes with season and over longer periods of time. Contributions to the scheme have helped to chart the increasing use of gardens by Goldfinches and Collared Doves, and to warn conservationists of the worrying declines in Song Thrushes, House Sparrows and Starlings (see page 15).

Weekly records collected by BTO/CJ Garden BirdWatchers show that Goldfinches make greatest use

ABOVE: unknown in Britain until the 1950s, the Collared Dove is now common and widespread, with gardens one of its preferred habitats.

of gardens during April. Interestingly, there is another slight peak in garden use at just the time that Goldfinches are laying their eggs, suggesting that females might be topping up on food at this time.

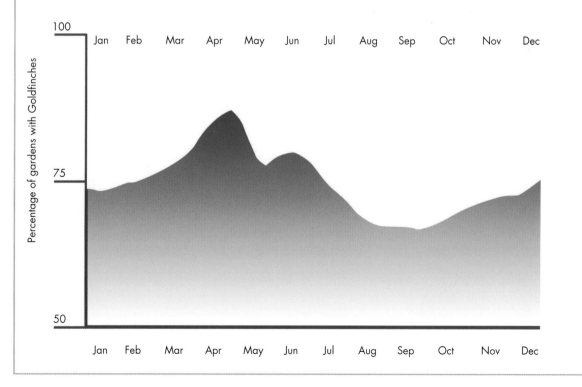

gardens is the beautiful Waxwing. These noisy, berry-raiding birds sometimes irrupt in large numbers from northern Europe. Their favourite food seems to be rowan and hawthorn berries, but cotoneaster berries and rosehips are among a myriad of others.

This is the time of year that birds tend to stick together to survive. Large mixed flocks of tits can be seen working through garden shrubs and birdfeeders. It is worth scanning

RIGHT: Fieldfares start to arrive from the Continent in October and stay all winter.

RIGHT: the smallest of Britain's common thrushes, the Redwing is another winter visitor which will visit gardens if food is in a short supply.

LEFT: large tit flocks flit through trees in winter; sometimes you will find a Treecreeper tagging along, using its long, decurved bill to extract insects from the bark of trunks and branches.

ABOVE: if you are really lucky you might find a rare wintering Firecrest mixed in with a tit flock. Its much more common relative, the Goldcrest, lacks the white supercilium and black stripe through the eye.

ABOVE: by putting out roosting pockets in the garden, you can really help small birds, such as Wrens, survive freezing night-time temperatures.

through these groups as sometimes other birds decide to tag on; Treecreepers and Goldcrests, for example, or if you are really lucky you might find a scarcity such as a Firecrest.

Developing as many winter roost sites as possible in your garden will not only help birds to survive, but is another way of attracting more species. Some birds survive extremely cold weather by roosting communally, including some species that are usually solitary, such as Wren. In fact, a single nestbox has been known to hold a staggering 60 Wrens. Long-tailed Tits also group together in large numbers and will use nestboxes and roosting pockets if available. Roosting pockets are quite cheap to buy and offer a safe, warm home for birds to escape the cold. Other birds such as Goldcrests and tits will also take advantage of these.

With nesting dates getting earlier and earlier, make sure that your nestboxes are clean and well-maintained before the end of January; and check before you move them in case you already have inhabitants inside.

Plants

With short daylight hours there are few flowering plants in the garden until February. Snowdrops break through frost-hardened ground as early as January, soon to be followed by Winter Aconites. There is still some controversy as to whether snowdrops are indigenous or introduced, but either way they are a welcome sight and an invaluable early source of nectar for newly emerged insects. There are more than 100 varieties of snowdrops and about 20 species, the Common Snowdrop perhaps being the best-known representative. Although the Winter Aconite is an introduced species, insects love it; the yellow bowl-shaped flowers allow them access to the stamens and therefore to a plentiful supply of pollen.

ABOVE: the noisy, high-pitched *tsee-tsee* contact calls often alert you to the presence of Long-tailed Tits before you see them.

ABOVE: only the female Holly bush bears berries.

Winter Heliotrope is a welcome garden escapee. Flowering from December to March, it has lovely fragrant, pale pink flowers and insects, especially bees, are attracted to its nectar. Crocuses also offer an early source of nectar and pollen and our native Stinking Hellebore attracts early bees with its unpleasant aroma. All hellebore species grow happily in partial shade.

Other plants that we commonly associate with winter, especially with December, are Mistletoe, Holly, Ivy and, of course, the Norway Spruce or Christmas tree. The first three are great for the garden and should be included if possible, but be careful if you decide to replant your Christmas tree outside as they can grow up to 30 m high. There are other, better conifers that you can plant, such as our three native species – Scots Pine, Yew and Juniper. Although the Yew's bright red berries are eaten by birds they are poisonous to

ABOVE: Mistletoe is a parasitic plant. It has around 200 host species but apple is the favourite, followed by poplar and lime.

ABOVE: beware of Yew trees in the garden, their poisonous berries can kill humans if eaten.

ABOVE: the Juniper is one of Britain's three native conifers; both the garden and wild varieties are great for larger gardens.

ABOVE: although Ivy can smother other trees, it is not a parasitic plant; it gets all its nutrients from soil via its roots.

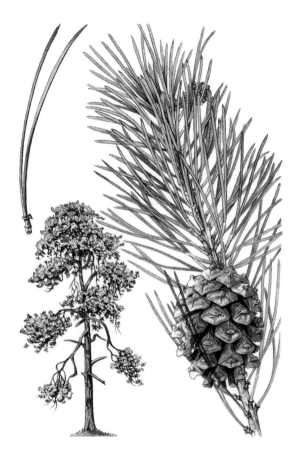

ABOVE: our traditional Christmas tree, the Norway Spruce was once native to Britain but became extinct here during the last Ice Age.

ABOVE: our native Scots Pine is a great conifer for large gardens but beware, it can grow up to 30 metres high.

mammals, so bear this in mind when planting it if you have children.

Holly is great for the garden, it can grow up to 15 m high and provide good cover for a variety of wildlife. Its winter berries are irresistible to birds but only the female tree produces them, so if your Holly is bare it is either a male or a female without a male close by.

Mistletoe is another famous berry that appears at this time of year. It is a parasitic evergreen shrub that grows high up on the branches of certain trees, especially fruit trees and lime; apple trees are its favourite host. Birds find the succulent, sugary flesh of the berries irresistible and they play a vital role in germination by wiping their bills on branches and through their seed-laden droppings. The seeds stick to

a branch, then send out little root-like stems that attach themselves under the bark.

Ivy is probably one of the most important native species to include in the garden. During winter this dense, evergreen climbing shrub offers garden wildlife great protection from the freezing weather. Its berries are a source of food for many birds, including Woodpigeons, Blackbirds and other thrushes. While other plants have shut down for winter, the Ivy's late flowering attracts a myriad of insects in search of their last nectar meal before hibernation; wasps, hoverflies, hornets, bumblebees and late-flying butterflies all benefit from this nectar-rich plant. In mild weather, Ivy can flower throughout the winter.

A sure sign that winter is nearing an end is the

RIGHT: the best way to identify Common Toads is by the warts all over their bodies. They also have a large paratoid gland behind the eyes. They produce strings of spawn that are wound around submerged plants.

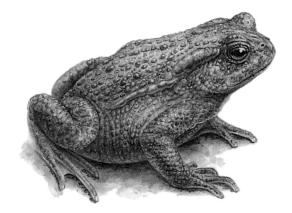

ABOVE: unlike toads, Common Frogs have smooth skin with no warts. At the end of winter, frogs and toads head for ponds to place their eggs as a mass of spawn.

emergence of Hazel catkins in February. These are the male flowers, while the females' are the tiny red tufts which, when fertilised, go on to become hazelnuts.

Reptiles and amphibians

Cold-blooded reptiles and amphibians remain inactive in winter. There is not enough heat in the sun to generate the energy required, so they hibernate. Rock and log piles near ponds offer frogs and newts a safe winter retreat. However, because our winters are getting warmer and shorter, certain amphibians are shaking off their torpor much earlier than normal. The Common Frog and Common Toad can be seen heading off to their spawning ponds as early as January. This is when our ponds and streams become steamy pools of passion, with fervid males gripping the females to death, sometimes literally. The males arrive first and start their familiar purring croak to attract the females. By February, if the weather is mild, ponds can be seen heaving with the gelatinous mass of frogspawn. It may look as though there is far too much for your pond to cope with, but do not be tempted to take it out as it is a great food source for other animals and it will settle down to its natural level.

LEFT: it does not take long for a freshly-made pond to become established. Usually the first guests will arrive within days of its completion.

ABOVE: the Brown-lipped Snail inhabits woodland, hedgerows and grassland and has adapted itself to survive in gardens. Its shell varies in colour from striped to plain brown, but the dark 'lip' distinguishes it from the similar White-lipped Snail.

It is too early for our reptiles to stir from their winter hibernation. If you are lucky you may have a Grass Snake hibernating under your compost heap or log pile.

Invertebrates

This is the quietest time of year for insects; some have laid eggs and died while others creep into crevices to sit out the cold weather. Some hibernators, such as caterpillars, snails, queen wasps and bumblebees and some butterflies have chemicals in their blood that act as an anti-freeze. Although it is very tempting to take a peak into one of the many insect boxes you have put in your garden, try to resist the urge; they probably will not survive through the remaining cold months if disturbed.

The first butterflies to take to the wing are usually the ones that have spent the winter as adults, including Red Admiral, Small Tortoiseshell, Brimstone and Peacock; most other butterflies spend the winter as caterpillars or pupae.

Want to help our butterfies and moths? Then become a member of Butterfly Conservation. By joining you are giving the movement moral support and democratic power. Visit the website www.butterfly-conservation.org to find out how.

RIGHT: because Red Admirals hibernate, they are among the first butterflies to emerge in spring, and increasingly they are appearing in late winter.

53

ABOVE: Hummingbird Hawkmoths get their name from their habit of hovering at flowers, sucking up nectar just like hummingbirds.

The queens of several species of bumblebee are out and about looking for a suitable nest site at this time. To combat the cold weather, they can increase their metabolic rate and therefore generate heat by flexing their flight muscles.

Look out for the white, fluffy cocoons tucked away in garden sheds or under logs. These silk-spun parcels can contain up to 1,000 spider's eggs. In some cases, the female spider dies after laying her eggs and spinning the egg-sac, leaving the tiny spiderlings to fend for themselves once they hatch in spring.

A Hummingbird Hawkmoth busily zipping in and out of the flowerbed may look like a fantastically rare and exotic bird visiting your garden. These are migrants that cannot survive our winters, so migrate to southern Europe. The influxes in late summer are from the emergence of successful breeding in the UK and it is thought that the early spring sightings are from the first migrants. However, there have been increasing numbers of sightings in February, suggesting that they may now be wintering in Britain.

RIGHT: the Small Tortoiseshell usually rests with its wings closed, opening and closing them rapidly to confuse predators.

SPRING
March to May

The dull, grey grip of winter begins to ease and March sees the first signs of spring bursting from our gardens. Insects will be flying, early-flowering hedges, trees and flowerbeds will be in bloom and birds will be at their most vocal. Many will be settling into their new territories to get on with the serious business of breeding. The longer daylight hours afford diurnal creatures more time to feed their young and provide more sunshine for plants to bask in. But March can sometimes have a nasty sting in its tail, and it can see temperatures ranging from below freezing to 20°C, while April may see more unpredictable weather with sunshine one minute and showers the next. Once the ground has warmed up, reptiles will make their first tentative steps out of hibernation.

Towards the end of spring, wildlife activity in the garden really gets into full swing, and it seems that every living thing is either fighting, flowering, feeding or mating.

LEFT: Elder blossom is a sign that spring is well and truly on its way. Blackthorn is usually the earliest of our native shrubs to blossom.

The garden

Spring is probably the busiest time in the garden. Insects move in en masse, enjoying their first feed on nectar-rich flowers. Overnight it seems that daffodils, crocuses, primroses, bluebells and other spring flowers have all burst into life. Water is getting warmer, bringing the first signs of life to resting ponds. It is not too late to put up any last-minute nestboxes for birds and, if you have not done so already, put up summer nursery bat boxes.

Birds will be belting out their songs, desperately trying to attract a mate and dashing around the garden defending territories. Take advantage of this by setting aside time to brush up on your birdsong skills. If you find a bird singing regularly from the same spot, you have probably found the centre of its territory, and once you have pieced together the territorial jigsaw puzzle, you can sit back and watch the antics of boundary disputes unfold.

Mammals

Badgers give birth in or around February but it takes a further nine or 10 weeks for the cubs to emerge from the sett. If the adults feel safe they will bring their cubs into gardens, especially if they are regularly fed. April or May is a great time to watch the cubs as they are busily distracted with the serious business of playing. The cubs stick with their mothers, learning which

ABOVE: Rabbits are gregarious so, if you seen one, you know that others will be nearby.

ABOVE: beware, playing fox cubs can cause havoc in the garden.

foods are good to eat, until they are about 15 weeks old, after which they have usually gained enough confidence to go foraging alone.

There is not much that these omnivores will not eat. Their diet consists of earthworms (about 80 per cent), slugs, small rodents, fruit, nuts (unsalted peanuts are an especially good way to tempt them into gardens), and grubs. It is best, though, to offer Badgers a mixture of food so as not to make them dependent upon one thing, as this can upset them if this food source is suddenly withdrawn. To keep your Badgers with you for longer, try smearing peanut butter onto logs – they will not be able to resist it.

Fox cubs first emerge from their earths in mid-April. The cubs are deaf, blind and unable to walk when they are born in March. They are born with blue eyes and chocolate-coloured fur. For the first 12 weeks, mothers rarely leave their cubs. After around four weeks the cubs feel sufficiently confident to wander on their own. If a vixen discovers something wrong with a cub, she will take it to the boundary of her territory and abandon it. However, if you find a young cub, do not assume that it has been abandoned – leave it for 24 hours and its parents will probably collect it. If it is still

ABOVE: the Stoat is probably the most successful rabbit deterrent you can get. Even the smaller Weasel will kill prey as large as a Rabbit.

LEFT: the Weasel is smaller than the Stoat and lacks its relative's black tail tip.

there after that, and looking sick or injured, contact your local vet or branch of the RSPCA.

When a Hedgehog wakes from hibernation in April there are two things on its mind – food and mating. Their courtship starts in May and is possibly the noisiest and most distressing thing you will hear in the garden during spring. You can be forgiven waking up in the middle of the night in a cold sweat thinking something dreadful is happening outside. Their courtship dance consists of the male and female circling one another, the female trying to keep her flank facing the male while resisting his amorous advances. This can sometimes last for hours if the female is not receptive. The loud snorting and snuffling noises escalate as the male gets more excited, if another nearby male hears this he too will want to join in, causing more noisy scuffles, but at least it gives the female a chance to slip away if she is not ready. The

babies, which are known as hoglets, are born a month after mating.

As the soil warms up, so does Mole activity, and molehills start to appear in the garden. It is best not to get upset over molehills as nothing really works as a deterrent and they are in fact good for the garden. They aerate the soil and the moles themselves will eat larvae, such as Cockchafers, which can harm bulbs. The blind and naked young are born towards late spring, deep down in an underground nest. In some cases, if the ground is prone to flooding for example, exceptionally large molehills called fortresses can be found. They contain their own network of tunnels, a nest and even a larder.

If you live in a rural area, you may see a Weasel dashing around the garden in early spring. This is a good sign as it means that your garden is part of a healthy habitat which supports enough mice and voles

RIGHT: molehills have their advantages; they aerate and till the soil, adding to its fertility.

getting involved
ARE BADGERS ABOUT?

Badgers are largely nocturnal, which means that they might be visiting your garden without your knowing about it, so look for the tell-tale signs of their presence. Damage to a lawn, caused by Badgers raking up the turf in search of earthworms, is characteristic, as are the shallow latrine pits that they dig. These pits will contain Badger droppings; oily in nature and smelling strongly of musk they often contain seeds and plant remains. Also look for Badger hairs caught on fences, where Badger trails may enter and leave the garden. The coarse hairs are 2-3 inches long.

ABOVE: Badgers have a hard time in Britain, even though they are protected under the Protection of Badgers Act 1992.

for weasels to predate. Sightings around this time of year are normally of males looking for receptive females to mate with. Normally they live in separate territories but these boundaries are forsaken during breeding. Stoats will also visit gardens. They look superficially similar to Weasels but are larger and have a black tip to the tail. Having said that, the males of both species are bigger than the females, so male Weasels can be the same size as female Stoats. If you suspect you have either of these mustelids in your garden, the best way to find out is to use a footprint tube (see page 32 for details).

Birds

Migration, migration, migration is the mantra for birds and indeed birdwatchers in spring. Now is the time that birds leave their winter retreats and return to their breeding sites. We say farewell to the flocks of Redwings, Fieldfares and other northern European birds that flew south to escape the cold winters and again welcome the hirundines and swifts that spent the winter in Africa. Sand Martins are usually the first to arrive, often by mid-March, with Swallows and House Martins, which are much more likely to be seen in and around gardens, following by the end of the month or during April. The larger, all-black, sickle-winged Common Swifts belong to a separate family – Apodidae – and first appear in numbers during late April with the bulk appearing in early May. Listen for their high-pitched screaming calls.

It is during this season that wind direction and the weather can influence the occurrence of certain birds, making it possibly the most exciting time for birdwatchers. Strong winds can blow migrating birds off course, so if you keep a garden list you may be able to add some unusual species. Remember to submit your recordings to the BTO's BirdTrack scheme (www.birdtrack.co.uk).

ABOVE: the Common Chiffchaff's familiar, repetitive *chiff-chaff* song can be heard as early as January. Although traditionally a summer visitor, increasing numbers are wintering in Britain.

There is a long tradition in Britain of recording the signs of spring, something that is known as 'phenology'. Whether it is the call of the first Cuckoo, the flowering of Hawthorn or the sighting of the first Brimstone butterfly, these signs of spring provide important markers of a changing climate. Instead of just keeping a note of these events in your nature diary, why not record them for 'Nature's Calendar' (www.naturescalendar.org.uk/) a national survey run by the Woodland Trust? You will be able to view your observations in a wider context and, at the same time, help researchers establish the effects of climate change on our wildlife.

getting involved
FINDING NEW ARRIVALS

Our summer migrants are arriving earlier now than they used to. Why not keep a record of when yours arrive, either in a diary or as part of the BirdTrack project (www.birdtrack.net)? See how yours compare with the national averages.

Sand Martin	25th March
Swallow	29th March
Yellow Wagtail	7th April
House Martin	8th April
Common Whitethroat	15th April
Sedge Warbler	16th April
Cuckoo	19th April
Turtle Dove	20th April
Common Swift	23rd April
Spotted Flycatcher	28th April

House Martins have a white throat and a white rump; they nest under the eaves of buildings.

Red throat, pale underparts and distinctive long tail-streamers help to identify the Swallow.

The first sign of Common Swifts in spring is often their screaming calls.

ABOVE: the clever and resourceful Magpie sometimes puts a roof over its nest to protect against predators and the elements.

RIGHT: female Great Spotted Woodpecker (left) lacks the red mark on the nape that is apparent in the male.

With experience and a good weather forecast you may be able to predict some of the scarce species of birds that might to turn up. For example, south-easterly winds in late March or early April can bring a scarcity such as a Black Redstart or Firecrest, particularly to gardens near the south or east coast. Common spring migrants that will be arriving in the garden from southern Europe and North Africa are Common Chiffchaff, Blackcap (although both species now regularly spend the winter in Britain) and Willow Warbler from late March and Cuckoo, Garden Warbler, Common and Lesser Whitethroats and Spotted Flycatcher from April.

As well as a host of newly arrived migrants, gardens across the country should be filled with the songs of both residents and summer visitors. The frantic drumming of Great Spotted Woodpecker can be heard as the male tries to attract a female. If you live in southern or eastern England you may be lucky enough to attract a Nightingale into your garden. Their powerful and melodious song consists of short, varied phrases of whistles, trills and rich warbling and once heard it is never forgotten.

ABOVE: Spotted Flycatchers arrive in May and leave by the end of August. Due to a dramatic drop in numbers, the species is becoming an unusual sight in gardens.

There are a couple of things you can do to detect which bird species you have nesting in or close to the garden. Try putting out some suitable nesting material and see which birds come to collect it. Sheep's wool, horse, human or pet hair from a brush, dry grass, moss, feathers and twigs can all be useful for nesting birds. You may be able to locate a nest if you keep an eye on the direction in which birds regularly fly. Many birds discard broken eggshells from their nests after hatching, so picking them up and identifying the fragments is a good way to see which species have hatched young.

One of the most impressive birds that can be regularly found in gardens is the Tawny Owl. It is our most common owl and a species that frequently uses nestboxes. The rather cute, downy owlets often leave the nest before they can fly and this does not mean that they have been abandoned. If you find one it should be left alone until the parent comes along to retrieve it and even persuade it to climb back into the nest.

ABOVE: Tawny owlet.
BELOW: provision of a large box can encourage Tawny Owls to nest in gardens.

ABOVE: Nightingales are rarely seen, preferring to skulk in the undergrowth. They arrive in April and leave around August to September and are rare visitors to gardens.

ABOVE RIGHT: the plain Garden Warbler's best distinguishing feature is its song, which consists of a pleasant warble which is rather like a scratchier version of the Blackcap's.

ABOVE: Blackcaps have a beautiful song and a distinctive call that sounds just like two stones being banged together. The female is similar to the male but has a brown cap.

Rowan

Horse Chestnut

Blackthorn

Plants

Towards the end of spring all traces of winter will have well and truly disappeared from the garden and it should be humming with life. The early flowering plants would have been a life-saver for early emerging pollen and nectar-feeding insects and trees that have shut down for winter are now awakening and bursting into blossom. Horse Chestnut trees are often the first to produce leaves – they appear from early April and the flowers follow soon after.

Willows, birches and oaks start to produce catkins, whose pollen is blown by the wind to fertilise the smaller female catkins. The nectar-rich catkins of our native sallow are the first to appear and can attract a wealth of insects, especially moths such as the Hebrew Character and Common Quaker. Elder leaves are present from March to November and flowers from June to July. Blackthorn can start to flower as early as February; this hardy shrub is impervious to the coldest of northerly winds and in defiance puts out an

Grey Sallow

Elder

ABOVE: Hawthorn traditionally blossoms in May, but the early appearance of the flowers in recent years could be linked to global warming.

Lesser Celandine

Ramsons

Cuckoo Pint

Primrose

ABOVE: Wild Cherry can grow up to 18 m high. It flowers in April and fruits in July.

impressive early blossom. Not only is its fruit, known as sloe berries, good for making sloe gin, but this thick, low-growing bush is great for nesting birds such as thrushes.

Other early flowering trees, which are great for insects and birds include Hawthorn, Wild Cherry and Rowan – the last has 28 species of insects associated with it. Although Hawthorn is commonly known as the May tree due to its May blossom, it now regularly flowers as early as March in southern England.

There are many spring-flowering plants that attract insects. Cuckoo Flower or Lady's Smock blooms from April to June and is attractive to Orange Tip and Green-veined White butterflies. It is not to be confused with the striking Cuckoo Pint or Lords and Ladies which flowers from April to June. The strong-smelling flower attracts insects, which then drop down into the

ABOVE: Stinging Nettles are an important food plant for the caterpillars of Small Tortoiseshell and Red Admiral butterflies.

flower's chamber, where they are trapped until they are covered in pollen, and released the next day. The 'pint' in their titles derives from the old English word 'pintle', meaning penis – hardly surprising considering their obvious phallic shape.

Primrose's nectar is found at the bottom of the flower tube, which means only long-tongued insects can reach the nectar. The name itself is derived from prima rosa, meaning 'first flower'. Early flying butterflies such as Brimstone are regular visitors to this delicate flower. Along with primroses, daffodils are another familiar sign of spring. Our native species, Wild Daffodil, used to grow commonly, so by planting this species we are helping to ensure its future survival. Bees and other insects are attracted to the nectar-filled cup at the base of the flower.

Other native plants that will attract insects are Lily of the Valley, Lesser Celandine, Lungwort and

ABOVE: the Common Frog is the most likely amphibian to appear in gardens, especially where there is a pond.

Ramsons. Great spring bloomers that are especially good for bumblebees are White Dead Nettle, Aubretia and flowering currants (*Ribes sp.*).

Reptiles and amphibians

Spring is a great time to watch reptiles. From April and even late March onwards they will be leaving their hibernation sites in search of warmth and food. As they are cold-blooded they need to warm up by basking in the sunshine. As the air temperature will still be relatively cool, they will need to bask for as long as they can, especially with the approach of the breeding season. Males will be more active as they go in search of suitable females. In early spring the best

ABOVE: snakes shed their skin several times a year. This one belonged to Britain's only venomous snake, the Adder.

ABOVE: the Common Toad prefers life out of water; it is only during the breeding season that it takes up residence in water.

time of day to spot them is between 11 am and 3 pm, but as the weeks pass they will bask earlier and earlier and even come out again in the afternoon.

Britain's only legless lizard, the Slow-worm, is the most frequently reported garden reptile. It is closely followed by the Grass Snake, which is especially fond of ponds that boast a bountiful supply of frogs. Common Lizards are not actually that common in gardens as they are usually habitat specific and tend to prefer heathland, moorland or rough grassland.

The best way to see reptiles is to put down corrugated iron sheets and see if they take refuge underneath.

From as early as March onwards that gelatinous mass of frogspawn will be hatching, Common Frogs can lay up to 2,000 eggs but only a small number will make it to maturity. The spawn and the tadpoles are vital food for a variety of species; even Blackbirds will

drop down to scoop up the tadpole surplus in ponds. After a sometimes very long walk to their breeding ponds, Common Toads lay long, single strands of toadspawn which are wrapped around pond weeds in shallow water. As the species is thought to be declining in Britain, probably due to water pollution, garden ponds are becoming more and more important for the Common Toad's survival.

As the water warms and the spawn hatches, our other native amphibians, the newts, leave their winter retreats on land and head for water, usually to the place that they were born. There are three species of newt in the UK, the Smooth Newt being the most common and frequently found in garden ponds. The smaller Palmate Newt looks very similar but prefers shallow ponds and acid soil and is therefore quite specific to this habitat.

Unlike the torrid frenzy of frog and toad mating, the behaviour of newts is far more sedate. Their

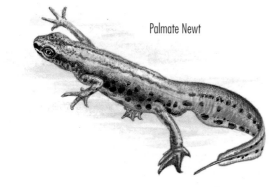

Palmate Newt

Smooth Newt

Great Crested Newt

Smooth and Palmate Newts can be very tricky to tell apart. The breeding males are most readily identified. Male Palmate Newts have black webbing between the toes on the hind feet, and look also for a narrow black filament protruding from the end of the tail. They also lack the crest of the breeding male Smooth Newt. Our rarest newt, the **Great Crested**, is still in decline and is therefore the least likely member of the family to occur in garden ponds. Beware of confusing breeding male Smooth Newts, which also have a crest, with Great Crested. The latter is always larger (15 cm long compared to 11 cm for Smooth Newt) and darker and often has rough skin.

Once you have identified your newt, report it to the National Amphibian and Reptile Recording Scheme (NARRS – www.narrs.org.uk), which runs the National Amphibian Survey and needs help with gathering information for all British species. You can also contact NARRS with details of frog or toad sites and for garden reptile sightings, which can be reported to the National Reptile Survey.

RIGHT: the filament at the tip of its tail identifies this newt as a Palmate.

ABOVE: planting nectar-rich plants can really help the survival of many of our insect species. Here a Brimsone butterfly feasts on a summer thistle.

elaborate courtship rituals are not only great to watch, but they are also unusual as no other amphibians practise such displays. Courtship starts with the male pursuing a female then swimming or 'dancing' in front of her while fanning its tail. The male is actually wafting glandular secretions her way and these stimulate the female to approach him. The male then places a parcel of sperm (spermataphore) in front of the female who then inserts it herself. The female lays up to 400 eggs on aquatic plants over the next few days. The newtlets or efts grow their front legs first and breathe through feathery gills.

Invertebrates

If you have a garden that is well-stocked with early flowering plants, by now you should be hearing the buzzing of insects. The first to be seen are usually those that have hibernated in or close to the garden, although warm southerly winds in early spring can bring in migrant species. Painted Lady butterflies and Dark Sword-grass moths have both been recorded as early as February. Butterflies that have spent the winter hibernating in or around the garden, such as Small Tortoiseshell, Brimstone, Peacock and Red Admiral, may have taken to the wing in February if it was warm enough.

Queen bumblebees are now digging their way out of their solitary hibernation chambers and the first thing they need to do is eat as much sugar-rich nectar and pollen as they can find. Soon they will be searching for nest-sites and laying eggs to begin the next generation. Queens are the only bees that survive

ABOVE: mating Blue-tailed Damselflies. As with all odonata species, the male holds onto the female after mating to prevent other males mating with her.

getting involved
MAPPING BEES

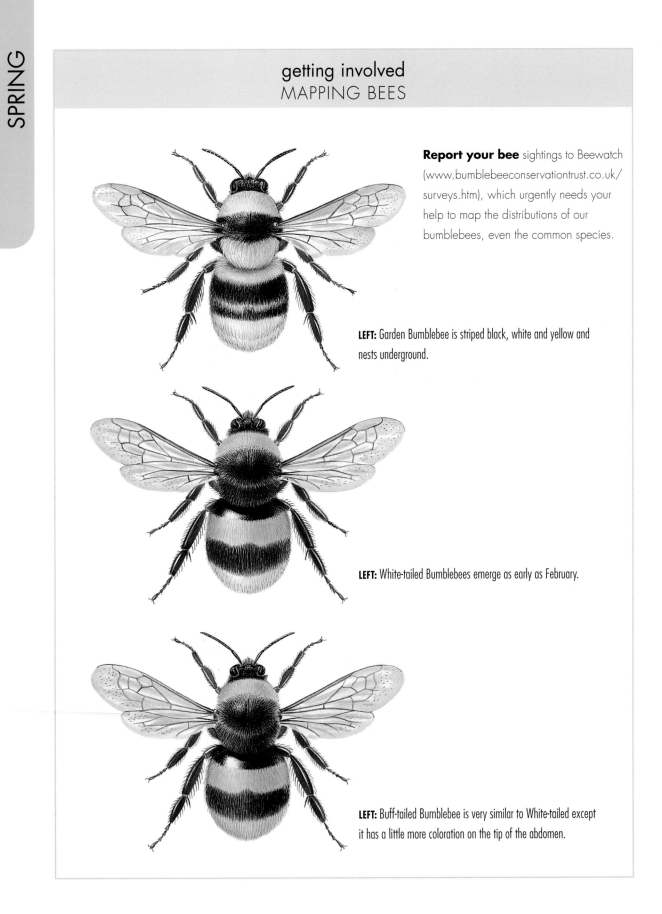

Report your bee sightings to Beewatch (www.bumblebeeconservationtrust.co.uk/surveys.htm), which urgently needs your help to map the distributions of our bumblebees, even the common species.

LEFT: Garden Bumblebee is striped black, white and yellow and nests underground.

LEFT: White-tailed Bumblebees emerge as early as February.

LEFT: Buff-tailed Bumblebee is very similar to White-tailed except it has a little more coloration on the tip of the abdomen.

ABOVE: Red-tailed is one of 25 species of bumblebee in the UK. Many of these need our help as several species are in severe decline.

getting involved
RECOGNISING DRAGONFLY CASES

Although adult dragonflies can be watched and identified when they visit your garden, it is often less apparent as to which ones will have used your pond for breeding. Fortunately, when dragonfly larvae emerge from a pond they have to shed their larval skin in order to gain their adult form. These skins can be found on waterside vegetation and, with a guide and a bit of effort, they can be identified. If you have a net, and fancy doing some pond dipping, then you should be able to catch some dragonfly larvae and identify these before they emerge.

RIGHT: dragonfly and damselfly larvae are voracious hunters, some of the larger species will even catch and eat small fish.

into spring as the rest of the colony dies out each winter. Buff-tailed and White-tailed Bumblebees are among the first to emerge, sometimes as early as February.

Most of our bees are solitary rather than colonial, and many of these species also take to the wing early. The Spring Flower Bee is one of the first to visit gardens each year. Also look out for the Cuckoo Bee which lays its eggs in the other bees' burrows. The Cuckoo Bee's young hatch quickly and eat the food supply intended for the young of their host.

Now is the time for the agile bumblebee mimics to

appear. Bee-flies are fast-moving balls of fur which hover in front of nectar-rich flowers, probing them with their long proboscis. These parasitic flies lay their eggs in the nests of solitary bees, the larvae then eat their hosts and all their food supplies. The first bee-fly likely to appear is the Large Bee-fly. Also keep an eye out for the rare Dotted Bee-fly. As the name suggests, it has rows of black spots on its wings.

From mid-April you may find strange, insect-shaped skins on emergent pond plants. These are the discarded skin casts, called exuviae, of the larvae of damselflies and dragonflies, of which there are about 15 British

ABOVE: the Broad-bodied Chaser flies from May to August and is a frequent garden pond visitor.

species that commonly occur in gardens. Both belong to the order Odonata which has been in existence for millions of years. Damselflies fold their wings close to their body while the wings of dragonflies remain fixed open at 90 degrees. The carnivorous larvae crawl up on tall pond plants, Yellow Flag iris being a favourite, but anything vertical may be used. First thing in the morning is the best time to see this and normally on a sunny day. Once out, the larvae perform their final moult, the skin splits and out pops a fully winged adult. The first damselflies to appear are often the Large Red Damselfly, Blue-tailed Damselfly and the superficially very similar Common Blue Damselfly and Azure Damselfly. Dragonflies tend to emerge a little later and include the chunky Broad-bodied Chaser and the impressive Emperor Dragonfly which, with a wingspan of 10.5 cm, is Britain's largest species.

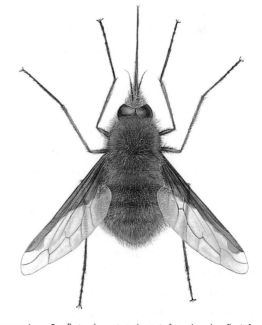

ABOVE: Large Bee-fly is a bee mimic that is in fact a harmless fly. It feeds from flowers from early spring.

SUMMER
June to August

Once summer arrives, gone are the frantic courtship and territorial bird battles of spring, while hibernating animals will have eaten enough to switch their minds to breeding and plants will be enjoying the warmer weather. The baby boom has arrived and our gardens will be acting as round-the-clock nurseries for an amazing number of species. June sees exhausted parent birds working until late, feeding their ever-demanding young, and by July the garden should be exuding the sweet, fragrant scents of summer which send insects into a dizzy spin as they gorge themselves on nectar and pollen.

The first signs of approaching autumn appear in early August, with the mass exodus of Common Swifts and later in the month with Swallows and House Martins lining up on telephone wires, waiting for the right time to depart for Africa.

LEFT: Hedgehogs have a varied diet, beetles are their favourite food but snails and slugs are also eaten.

ABOVE: the first generation of Holly Blue butterflies is on the wing from April to May, with a second emerging in August.

The garden

Summer is possibly the best time of the year to remind yourself that gardening really is worthwhile. However, towards the end of summer the garden can look rather ravaged, especially if it is extremely parched. As drier and hotter summers are becoming more frequent, it may be a good idea to plant more Mediterranean plants, such as wormwood, aubretia and cistus, which are more easily able to thrive in hot, dry conditions. With or without a hose-pipe ban, collecting your own rainwater should be a priority for any wildlife gardener. Adding rainwater to ponds can help reduce the risk of green algae, as tap water contains minerals that feed the algae.

Mammals

If you have struck up a good relationship with your visiting or resident garden mammals (or to put it another way – if you feed them regularly) there is a good chance they will bring along their offspring. Now is a good time to see Fox cubs; not only have they gained in size but also in confidence, so by summer they spend much time playing and mock hunting, which in turn teaches them vital survival skills. If you have a large garden, you may have the foxes' earth (underground burrow) within your boundary. Likely spots are under sheds or tree trunks or in hollow trees, while in some cases they will take over disused Badger setts.

ABOVE: Red Valerian is one of the best plants you can put in your garden to attract butterflies and moths, especially the Hummingbird Hawkmoth.

This may not be good news to some people as foxes can cause chaos in the garden. Holes in lawns and flowerbeds, piles of smelly faeces as they mark their territory, noisy contact calls and very nervous chickens are just some of the things to expect if you are living with foxes. However, all these can pale into insignificance in June, when the cubs abandon their earths for the great outdoors and have a habit of chewing anything that is left lying around, flattening flowerbeds and leaving half-eaten animal remains in the garden. But who cares? Having these fantastic, intelligent, wild animals sharing our space offers hours of entertainment, not to mention free pest control.

Although the Edible Dormouse is undoubtedly cute, this species can be a mixed blessing if it takes up residence in your home. It was first introduced into Britain in 1902 as part of a wildlife collection in Tring, Hertfordshire. Inevitably some escaped and started to breed successfully in the wild. There are now thought to be about 10,000 Edible Dormice in the Chilterns and the species is slowly expanding its range. Otherwise known as the 'fat dormouse' (the Romans used to fatten them up and eat them), this close relative of our native Common Dormouse can cause considerable damage to homes. They have taken to nest-building in roof spaces and have a nasty habit of gnawing through electric cables. The fact that they strip bark from young trees and eat birds' eggs does not help their public relations campaign. If you find Edible Dormice in your loft or shed, remember that this is a protected species, so you will need advice if you want them removed.

The Common Dormouse is in fact one of the rarest mammals to visit British gardens and it is a rapidly declining species. To stand any chance of attracting one you must first live near a large area of ancient woodland with a plentiful supply of its favourite food – hazelnuts. You will also need to live in southern England as the further north you travel the rarer they become; the species is absent altogether from Scotland and Northern Ireland.

Common Dormice are undoubtedly very cute, with their furry tails, big dark eyes and golden fur. Owing to their nocturnal habits and hibernation from October to March or April, it is extremely difficult to see these shy animals in the wild. The closest you are likely to get is finding the remains of nibbled hazelnut shells

ABOVE: although localised to a small area of southern England, there are signs that the introduced Edible Dormouse's distribution is slowly spreading.

ABOVE: during the summer months Foxes can look remarkably lean owing to the moulting of their thick winter coats.

and stripped hazel bark from the base of trees. The hazelnut shells resemble miniature clogs as the dormice invariably tackle the nut from the blunt end, making a round hole with teeth marks on the outer edge, but perfectly smooth inside. Wood Mice, Bank Voles and squirrels also break open nuts in a similar fashion – see www.greatnuthunt.org.uk for an identificaton guide to the nibbled shells.

If you are lucky enough to have Common Dormice nearby, you may just be able the encourage them to hibernate in your garden. Erecting specially made nestboxes will certainly help, although there are records of winter nests being made in Pampas Grass and in garden sheds

Although bats actually mate during autumn or winter, the females do not become pregnant until the following spring. They are able to store the sperm in their bodies until needed; this method is called delayed implantation. Babies (usually one but sometimes two) are born in the summer, and the species most likely to share your garden or house are Common Pipistrelle, Soprano Pipistrelle and Brown Long-eared Bat. During the summer, these species use our roof spaces or boxes as nurseries. If you have bats in your home, remember they are all protected species and that any attempt to harm them is a criminal offence. The damage they cause is minimal, and when they leave at the end of summer, a quick brush to remove the tiny guano pellets is all that is necessary. The benefit of having these mobile midge removers in your garden far outweighs the negatives. Baby bats are born blind, hairless and helpless, they suckle from their mother and rely heavily on warmth to grow and stay alive.

If you live in certain parts of Ireland and Scotland, the Scottish Highlands in particular, you may be familiar with the Pine Marten. The blind and hairless

ABOVE: the tiny Muntjac, also known as the 'barking deer' was introduced from Asia to Woburn, Bedfordshire, in the early part of the last century and has spread to many counties in southern England, where it frequently visits rural and suburban gardens.

RIGHT: Scotland's western Highlands are the best place to see Pine Martens — they are frequent visitors to birdtables in some areas.

baby martens are born in spring, but by mid-June they start to emerge from their den, although they never venture far from their mothers. Visits to gardens can be a regular event in areas where they are locally common and humans are tolerant. There is also a small population in northern England but its distribution is sporadic.

Baby Hedgehogs can be seen from mid- to late spring through to autumn. The risk of late-born hedgehogs not surviving the winter is higher as there is a greater chance that they will not have eaten enough to get them through hibernation.

Although it seems incongruous to see deer trotting along the pavement in a town, they frequently visit built-up areas to feed on garden plants. The two species most likely to be found in gardens are our

ABOVE: Sparrowhawk is an impressive hunter which regularly raids gardens; 98 per cent of its diet made up of birds.

native Roe Deer and the introduced Muntjac. Munjacs breed throughout the year but this is a busy season for the Roe Deer. Their 'rut' starts in June, with mating following from July to August, although this would be a truly remarkable record if it did happen in the average garden. Delayed implantation means that young (occasionally twins) are born the following May or June.

Birds

Now is the time to spare a thought for the exhausted birds that have been working tirelessly to feed and protect their young. Some birds will be onto their fourth brood, so there is little wonder that some plumages will be looking a bit shabby. Towards the end of summer birds undergo their annual moult, swapping their old worn-out feathers for newer, brighter ones. Juveniles will lose their first feathers and moult into their adult plumage.

It is a mistake to think that birds do not need feeding during the summer months; in fact both the RSPB and BTO recommend that you do. If anything, now is the time they could really do with a helping hand. While feeding young, Blue Tits have been recorded taking a quick break from finding insects by helping themselves to a quick snack from a peanut feeder.

Feeding birds live food such as mealworms at this time of year can offer an essential protein boost. It may seem strange to be opening a tin of cat food for your birds but at this time of year this meaty treat will be greedily snatched from the table by Blackbirds – they will even bring their young to the table to feast on it. Perhaps the most important thing for birds at this time of year is a simple bowl of life-saving water. Rainwater is best but during the dry, drought-ridden days of summer, anything will do. As soon as birds realise they have a constant supply of water (do not forget to keep it topped up) they will be regular visitors.

Brown Long-eared Bat (above) and
Common Pipistrelle (right) are two of the
bat species most likely to visit gardens,
both often using roofs as temporary homes.

LEFT: the Noctule bat is one of the
Britain's largest. It can often be seen
hunting over hedgerows and forest,
and sometimes over gardens.

SUMMER

ABOVE: Robins in the garden can become very tame, which can be fatal if there are cats around.

ABOVE: the bright pink-and-blue plumage of the male Chaffinch makes it a truly spectacular bird.

Of course, the presence of naïve fledglings in the garden means that predators will be lining up for an easy meal. The biggest problem is cats, which kill more garden birds than any wild predator. A natural killer is the Sparrowhawk, which is so called because birds (not just sparrows) make up 98 per cent of its diet. Sparrowhawks are perfectly designed, their short, rounded wings enabling them to twist and turn around trees and other obstacles in pursuit of their prey. As easily as a Blackbird will gobble down a worm, a Sparrowhawk can pluck a bird from a feeder. This is one reason why placing a birdfeeder near cover is a good idea.

It is worth remembering that various scientific surveys show there is no evidence to suggest that natural predation, whether it is by Sparrowhawks, Magpies or other species, is having any effect on the demise of some of our songbirds. Changing habitats, problems abroad in wintering sites and modern farming systems are more likely culprits.

By late summer look out for birds you do not often see in the garden, as some migrants readily adapt to the garden environment. Tiny Willow Warblers and Common Chiffchaffs are great to watch as they diligently move through bushes in search of insects. Look at Collared Doves carefully in case you have a visit from the rather shy but breathtakingly beautiful Turtle Dove.

Plants

By now the garden really should be looking and smelling beautiful. By cleverly planting a selection of flowers that smell best in the evening, you can attract a range of interesting moths, which in turn will attract bats; the ensuing aerial combats will be well worth all that hard graft in the garden.

Plants that are especially good in the evening are Night-scented Stock, which attracts Common Blue butterflies as well as moths, and Tobacco Plant which is a semi-evergreen plant with long, tubular flowers and is a good source of nectar for moths. Red Valerian is an excellent insect plant, which is especially good for migrant Hummingbird Hawkmoths and Silver-Y Moths. Evening primroses have wonderful sweet

ABOVE: fledgling Blackbirds are voracious carnivores, and leaving out trays of cat food for them is a good way to help their parents with the feeding.

ABOVE: Buddleia is such a good butterfly plant it is also called the 'butterfly bush'.

fragrances and are ideal for planting in pots if space is limited, especially species such as Common Evening Primrose. Summer Jasmine is one of the most fantastic, sweet-smelling, pungent fragrances you can find, and many moths would readily agree. Climbing plants such as our native Honeysuckle produce a heady scent that attracts many insects, including hawkmoths and White Admiral butterflies, while the aphids it attracts also draw in lacewings and ladybirds. Birds nest in its dense foliage and eat its autumn berries.

ABOVE: Honeysuckle is attractive to all sorts of insects.

ABOVE: the Painted Lady butterfly is a long-distance migrant that flies to Britain from the Mediterranean.

There are many summer-flowering plants that are popular with insects, and some can flower throughout spring, summer and autumn, including California lilac and Hebe species. Soapwort attracts many moths, especially hawkmoths, and is also good to plant as slugs and snails tend to avoid it. They will also stay clear of Foxglove which, as its scientific name Digitalis purpurea suggests, is the natural source of the drug Digitalis that is commonly used to treat heart conditions. Various species from the onion family are good at attracting insects, including hoverflies, bees,

Aubretia

Red Valerian

Evening Primrose

Dog Rose

Viper's Bugloss

ABOVE: Foxglove may look like a colourful garden hybrid but it is a native British plant commonly found in woodlands.

ABOVE: cultivating a wildflower meadow is a great way to attract an incredible variety of wildlife to your garden.

ABOVE: carefully check the recesses of flower-heads and you may find a crab spider lying in wait for a visiting bee or fly.

butterflies and moths, with Mouse Garlic and Ornamental Onion being two great garden varieties.

The bright purple-blue flowers of Verbena are popular with butterflies, especially Peacocks, and no wildlife garden should be without Viper's Bugloss, which is so called as it was once used as a remedy for viper bites. This is perhaps the best plant for attracting bumblebees into your garden. Without doubt, the most popular insect plant must be Buddleia, which is commonly called 'butterfly plant' – there are many

varieties and all are great for insects.

For a dash of native pink in the garden, plant a mallow shrub. If you look closely into the pale pink flowers, you may just find a patient crab spider such as *Misumena vatia* waiting to pounce on a visiting hoverfly.

As well as an essential culinary requirement, planting a herb garden is a great way to attract insects. Consider Lavender, Rosemary, Sage, Catmint, Wild Basil, Wild Marjoram and Chives. The beauty of

ABOVE: juvenile newts have feathery-looking, external gills just behind their eyes.

planting herbs is that you do not need a large garden or even a garden at all, as they are perfect for pots and window boxes.

Reptiles and amphibians

By now reptiles should be in their element as July is officially the hottest month in Britain. Common Lizards give birth to live young which are born in late July or August. They are encased in a membranous sac, which they pierce with a special egg-tooth and they are independent from the moment they are born. Slow-worms give birth to between six and 12 live

young during August or September.

Many people believe that newts spend all their time in water, but in fact they spend more time out of the water than in it. Newts come out of hibernation in late March or April and head straight for water to breed, and by the end of June most of the mating has finished. Although some spend the rest of the summer in ponds, others decide to feed on land instead. It is during these excursions that they can be mistaken for lizards. By the end of summer the Smooth Newt's feathery-gilled tadpoles or efts mature, becoming miniature versions of the adults. As well as the adults,

ABOVE: despite its name the Common Lizard is generally a rare visitor to gardens. This individual is in the process of growing a new tail.

ABOVE: although it appears snake-like, the Slow-worm is in fact a legless lizard.

they too leave the water at the end of summer. Females lay up to 400 individual eggs but, on average, only six reach maturity. Typical newt predators are Grass Snakes, Blackbirds, Hedgehogs and even other efts. The same heavy death toll applies to froglets and toadlets. It can be carnage at grass-cutting time as thousands are mown to pieces across the country as they hide in the long grass, avoiding their many predators.

Invertebrates

Attracting hoverflies into the garden can only be a good thing. They are completely harmless, simply mimicking the wasp's striped coat to make themselves look more menacing. The larvae feed on aphids and other plant pests. The female lays her eggs near to the aphids, so that when the larvae hatch a few days later

they can start to feed straight away. There are around 50 typical garden species including our largest hoverfly, *Volucella zonaria*, and the common *Eristalis tenax*, *Syrphus ribesii* and *Episyrphus balteatus*, also the Woolly Hoverfly *Criorhina floccosa* and *Volucella pellucens*, *Epistrophe grossulariae* and *Helophilus pendulus* among many others. Planting Pot Marigold and Angelica will encourage hoverflies into the garden.

The familiar ladybird is a beetle that gardeners welcome with open arms. The carnivorous adults and young of the various species feast on large numbers of insect pests, including greenfly, mites, mealy bugs and small caterpillars. Ladybird larvae look nothing like adults – these 'insect alligators' have segmented bodies with large jaws and are dark grey-blue with pale orange or white markings.

ABOVE: ladybird pupae look quite different from the adult insects and tend to be much less conspicuous.

ABOVE: there are 46 species of ladybird in Britain and the Two-spot is one of the most common.

ABOVE: the Seven-spot Ladybird is another widespread species that is commonly found in gardens.

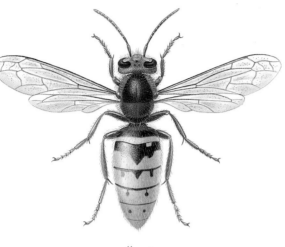

Hornet

Common Wasp

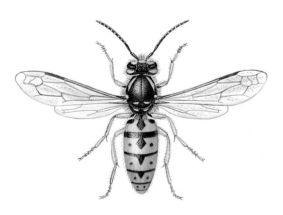

German Wasp

It would not be summer without the inevitable panic and undeserved culling of the fabulous wasp. Wasps are fascinating animals that need all the help they can get. After all, they help us in the garden by killing a huge number of insects that could otherwise harm plants. We have nine species, but the two most likely to occur in gardens are the Common Wasp and German Wasp. The first thing the queen wasp does after hibernation is build an intricate 'paper' nest, which is constructed from chewed wood. She then lays her eggs and tends the hatched grubs, feeding them with insects. Once these female, sterile workers mature, they help the queen tend the successive generations. Towards the end of summer, the queen produces males

ABOVE: this bumblebee hoverfly is a remarkable mimic. Although it has no sting, its fat, hairy body and black, yellow and white stripes are enough to warn off many predators.

Probably the most impressive and rarest beetle you can find in the garden, but only if you live within its limited range in southern Britain, is the Stag Beetle. Males have large, showy mandibles that resemble a stag's antlers; although they look terrifying, these harmless beetles are vegetarians that feed mainly on tree sap. Females lack the large 'antlers' but still have a set of sharp mandibles which are used for excavating soil and rotten wood. Males use their 'antlers' during courtship battles.

Rotten log piles and old tree stumps are the best garden homes you can offer Stag Beetles, which are increasingly localized and scarce. Report any sightings of these magnificent insects to www.ptes.org/greatstaghunt.

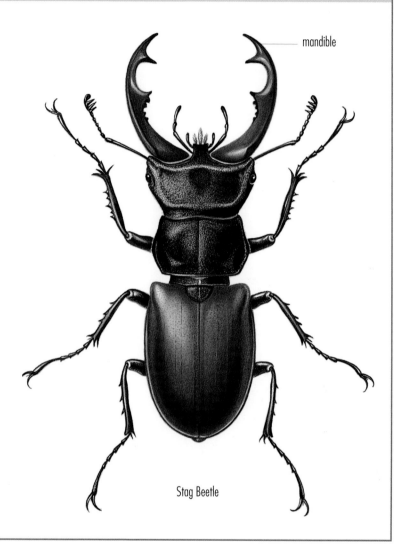

mandible

Stag Beetle

(drones) and females (queens). Both leave the nest to mate with other wasps, and the workers and drones die, leaving the fertile queens to hibernate over winter. With all this activity, wasps are far too busy to bother attacking humans; the only thing on their minds is to find food for the colony. It is only towards the end of the summer, once the colony stops producing young, that the workers head for our picnic tables in search of sugary foods. Normally they eat a sugary secretion made by the grubs, so once that is withdrawn you have to feel sorry for these poor wasps as they tear around in desperate need of a sugar fix.

The Hornet is our largest wasp species. It has chestnut-brown markings instead of black, and behaves in a much more docile manner than the Common Wasp, so it, too, is harmless unless provoked.

AUTUMN
September to November

Animals, insects, birds and plants should all be getting ready for the oncoming coldest months of the year, although strange things are undoubtedly happening in Britain as a direct result of warmer winters. Hedgehogs have been recorded out and about on Christmas Day, Swallows have turned up in February and records show that dormice are hibernating five and a half weeks less than they did 20 years ago.

For some it is a good thing: fewer birds freeze to death and food is more plentiful, but for others, such as our hibernating mammals, it can be devastating. Warm spells can speed up their metabolism, causing them to wake up, which can exhaust their vital fat and energy levels necessary for their survival through to spring.

The threat of winter is still too great for our garden wildlife to ignore, which is why autumn is such a great season to sit back and watch the frantic preparations unfold.

LEFT: autumn sees Coal Tits wander into many gardens from their woodland breeding territories. The long white nape-patch and grey and buff tones of their plumage enable them to be easily distinguished from the commoner green, yellow and blue Great Tit.

The garden

By the end of September the garden will be losing its buzz as insect numbers diminish; colourful flowers are replaced by seeds, fruits and nuts; and leaves are ridding themselves of moisture, replacing greens with autumnal reds, browns and yellows. The wildlife gardener has plenty of preparation work to do. Hedge and conifer trimming, the final grass cut for late-flowering meadows, tidying up the pond and setting aside various areas for hibernation sites. Do not be too eager to dead-head every plant, as leaving seed-heads and allowing vegetation to die back naturally will offer a great source of food and shelter for birds and insects. Piles of leaves are a great natural home for a variety of garden wildlife. If you have planted well you should have a berry bonanza in the garden which will attract flocks of ravenous thrushes, Blackbirds and, if you are really lucky, maybe even a Waxwing. Our lawns and borders become precious pantries for birds as they stash seeds and fruits for colder weather.

ABOVE: autumn is the prime season for fungi and many species, including Brown Mottlegill, appear in gardens.

RIGHT: although in serious decline in most of England and Wales, the Red Squirrel is still widespread and common in parts of Scotland.

ABOVE: forward-thinking Grey Squirrels make a stash of food in autumn to see them through periods of bad winter weather.

Mammals

With summer over, breeding finished and the young independent, now is the time for mammals to concentrate on preparing for their toughest season of the year. Some sensibly decide to opt out of winter altogether and go into hibernation. Towards the end of autumn, summer coats have been replaced by thicker winter fur, making animals look almost twice their size. The Red Squirrel's winter coat is usually a much darker red, with large, striking ear tufts that offer vital protection for these vulnerable extremities. Only a lucky few will enjoy Red Squirrels in the garden as their range is now restricted to mainly mature conifer and some deciduous forests in Scotland, Ireland and Wales. There are still a few remnant populations left in England and reintroduction schemes are pushing their numbers up.

The introduced Grey Squirrel receives constant bad press. Whether it is due to pushing out our native Red Squirrel (there is still no conclusive evidence that this is the case) or raiding birds' nests, you have to admire its amazing ability to adapt. It has an extremely varied diet and adapts to different habitats with ease. Its winter dreys are larger and less flimsy than those used in summer and these substantial, football-sized balls of leaves and twigs are usually placed on a branch close to the trunk. During cold spells they will curl up and sleep through, venturing out occasionally to dig up hidden food.

For our garden rodents, prolonged freezing weather can be fatal. Small mammals such as shrews and voles need to eat every two to three hours just to survive, and during cold weather they need to eat around the clock. They are too small to hibernate as they are unable to hold sufficient fat reserves. The Pygmy Shrew is Britain's smallest mammal, although it is usually the Common Shrew that you find abandoned by cats due to the apparent foul taste of their flesh.

From September onwards, some rodents are on the look-out for better, warmer homes. The Wood Mouse

Wood Mouse

Pygmy Shrew

Common Shrew

Yellow-necked Mouse

ABOVE: most gardens in the UK will hold at least one of the above species.

and the larger Yellow-necked Mouse will take advantage of available space in lofts, sheds and outhouses to see out the winter. You can often tell what species you have in the garden from their food remains. Each rodent has its own particular way of eating hazelnuts: squirrels split them open lengthways, Bank Voles take off the top, dormice make a smooth-edged hole in the side, while Wood Mice make a similar hole but with tooth-marks.

Bats start to hibernate in November, with both species of pipistrelle and Brown Long-eared Bat the main garden visitors, although several other species have been recorded. Now is the time to put up boxes for winter roosts, although cellars, outhouses and roof spaces are often preferred.

Towards the end of autumn, Stoats can go so far as to completely change their colour in preparation for winter. This only happens with northern populations where the characteristic white coat and black tip to the tail can be seen.

If your garden backs on to woodland or open fields there is a chance that you may hear the prehistoric bellows and grunts of the Red Deer rut. It is in fact Roe Deer that are more likely to visit your garden, although they already had their rut in July and August. Instead of hibernating, Badgers tend to sleep a lot more,

ABOVE: the impressive Waxwing is an irregular late autumn and winter visitor to Britain. Depending upon food supplies in Scandinavia, where the species breeds, there can be large influxes one year and hardly any the next.

Tawny Owls are noisy neighbours and their well-known *kee-wick* and hooting calls can be heard from late autumn. Calling activity varies with season and is most obvious in November. It is usually heard from an hour or so after dusk and can continue right through the night, as the owls proclaim ownership of their territory. Calling behaviour is greatly reduced on wet or windy nights because the owls know not to waste their efforts when weather conditions may reduce how far their calls carry. Keep a simple weekly record of when, and at what time, you hear Tawny Owls calling and do not forget to note down what the weather was doing.

RIGHT: Tawny Owl is Britain's most common owl and the one most likely to appear in gardens.

especially in very cold weather, which is why they need to eat as much as possible in autumn to see them through.

Birds

Just as many of our breeding birds will be heading south in search of warmer weather, some of those that spent the summer further north in Europe will be heading our way. Birds that rely on insect food, such as Swallows, House Martins, warblers and flycatchers are leaving for Africa, while berry-eating birds such as thrushes start migrating south to take advantage of our milder winters and bountiful berry bushes.

Sometimes vast numbers of birds will turn up in autumn; these occurrences are called 'irruptions' and usually happen when their normal food source fails. The stunning Waxwing is an uncommon winter visitor but when they do irrupt, large flocks will descend on berry bushes in any location, even supermarket car parks and city centres.

Common winter visitors include Redwing and Fieldfare, while our resident populations of Mistle and Song Thrushes swell as more arrive from the Continent. This is an exciting time for birdwatchers and almost anything can turn up. For example, strong westerly winds can push American songbirds across the Atlantic and exceptional British garden records in autumn and early winter include American Robin and Baltimore Oriole. And it is not just birds that can be blown off course in this way – insects such as the Monarch Butterfly sometimes make the crossing too.

As many of our resident birds are joined by their European counterparts, competition at garden feeders can become quite intense. To lessen the squabbles it may be a good idea to provide more than one feeder. Numbers of Siskins swell as resident birds are joined by migrants. Scrutinising Chaffinch flocks at this time of year may pay dividends as they often contain wintering Bramblings – the two species often join

ABOVE: Song Thrush numbers swell in autumn as resident birds are joined by those fleeing the harsh weather in northern Europe.

forces and regularly feed together on beechmast. As well as the bounty of berries, seeds and nuts, gardens with fruit trees will offer valuable food if some windfalls are left on the ground, with thrushes and Blackbirds especially likely to benefit.

Plants

The aim for plants this season is to get their seeds dispersed and germinated as quickly as possible. Some wrap them up in colourful, juicy flesh in the form of berries and dangle them voluptuously to entice animals. For any animal or bird wanting to gain extra weight for the winter, this timing is perfect. The seeds are then ejected in faeces away from the plant, so the

ABOVE: although predominantly insectivorous, the Blue Tit also feasts on berries when available.

ABOVE: competition at the feeders grows as the new winter arrivals join our existing Siskin flocks.

RIGHT: a close relative of the Chaffinch, Bramblings spend the winter in Britain and are often attracted to feed on beechmast.

seedling is less likely to compete with its parent. Others attach wings to the seeds so they can fly when they fall, and some just let them drop and wait for animals to bury them in the hope that they will forget where they have left them.

Every great wildlife garden has a plentiful supply of colourful, berry-producing plants. Some great red-berry plants are Hawthorn, Rowan, Dog Rose, Spindle, Cotoneaster, Firethorn, Black Bryony, Woody Nightshade and Yew.

The Blackthorn bush produces bluish-black berries called sloes, which are great for making sloe gin if you can get there before the birds. Elder and Buckthorn berries are black, while the Alder Buckthorn's berries turn from green to red to dark purple. Buckthorn is an important all-year-round plant for bees, birds and butterflies, especially Brimstones.

The name snowberry perfectly describes the bright-

ABOVE: Bramble patches in the garden can provide food and shelter for a terrific amount of wildlife, while humans are also partial to their blackberries.

ABOVE: the familiar, winged seeds of the Sycamore provide autumn food for birds, mammals and insects.

white berries produced by the bushes of the genus *Symphoricarpos*. Not only do they look stunning, but the berries and in fact the whole plant benefit a multitude of wildlife.

As well as our native fruit trees such as Crab Apple, Wild Plum (or Bullace) and the cherry trees, Wild Cherry and Bird Cherry, all fruit trees will be welcome news to your garden animals. It is not only birds and mammals that feed from them, they are also a crucial food source for late-flying insects. You never know, if your fallen fruit attracts large numbers of bees, you may just attract the rare and exotic-looking European Bee-eater. These very rare migrants overshoot from their usual breeding grounds on the Continent and turn up especially in autumn and spring.

Brambles might be a nightmare for some gardeners, but for wildlife they offer protection and a great autumnal larder. Late-flying butterflies such as the

Comma, Peacock and Red Admiral feed from the fruit along with mammals such as voles and mice.

The familiar Sweet Chestnut tree is not native to Britain but was probably brought by the Romans from the Mediterranean region. The male and female flowers are on the same upright stalk and rely totally on insects for pollination. Chestnuts ripen in September and are loved by animals such as squirrels and voles. The chestnuts we roast on open fires tend to come from southern Europe. Even our much-loved Horse Chestnut tree is not native – it was introduced in the late 16th century from the Balkans. This does not affect its benefit to British wildlife as the flowers are a good source of pollen for insects and the familiar 'conker' not only passes many an hour in the playground but provides a nutritional meal for deer and rodents.

Probably the most important tree for wildlife in

ABOVE: Hornbeam seedcases are also winged to help with dispersal, but the wings do not taper near to the base like those of the Sycamore.

ABOVE: Common Ash grows up to 40 m high and is another tree that produces winged fruit.

Bird Cherry

Sweet Chestnut

Spindle

Alder Buckthorn

Britain is the oak. Hundreds of species benefit from the oak tree and some 350 insect species have been recorded on it, including 150 types of aphid alone, along with 30 species of lichen. The fruit, more commonly known as the acorn, is an invaluable food source from September through to November. In a bumper year a mature tree can produce up to 50,000 acorns; these 'mast years' are much appreciated by Jays and squirrels, which rely heavily on this fruit. Oak trees and animals have a symbiotic relationship: as the acorns are too heavy to be taken by the wind, the oak relies on these animals for dispersal. Autumn sees some frantic behaviour as Jays and squirrels race around the garden gathering acorns and stashing them for winter. Fortunately for the oak tree, many of these are misplaced, leaving the usually single seed within to grow.

There are lots of seeds flying around in autumn – literally; the seeds of many trees, such as Hornbeam, Sycamore and Field Maple, have wings attached to catch the wind and help with dispersal. Look out for thistledown as it floats across the garden, each seed held by a parachute of pappus; Goldfinches are particularly fond of these seeds. The familiar bunches of winged Ash seeds can be seen dangling from the trees way after all the leaves have fallen. Letting plants go to seed is a great way of feeding birds for free. Some good autumn seed-heads include *Miscanthus*, perennial grasses, pampas grass and Love-in-a-mist.

Along with many animals, Chaffinches and winter visiting Bramblings will be taking advantage of the fruit or 'mast' from the Beech. In autumn the scaly cup slits into four, releasing two three-sided nuts.

ABOVE: also known as Mountain Ash, the Rowan is one of Britain's best native berry-producing trees.

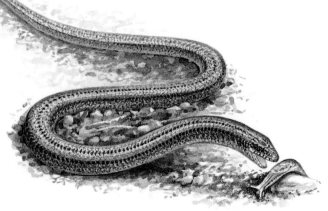

RIGHT: Grass Snake eggs hatch during early autumn, each clutch releasing up to 40 independent snakelets.

Reptiles and amphibians

Our three species of newt need to hibernate in a relatively warm, frost-free place from late October or November until spring and now is a good time to spot them as they head off in search of suitable sites. Smooth, Palmate and Great Crested Newts only visit water in spring in order to breed, although some young adult males may stay put, hibernating in the mud at the bottom of their breeding ponds.

By the end of September the eggs of our largest reptile have hatched. Female Grass Snakes typically grow to 130 cm and males to about 100 cm, although larger specimens have been recorded. Females lay between eight and 40 eggs in a warm, dark place; compost heaps and log piles are ideal sites. Occasionally Grass Snakes nest communally, some of these nests holding up to 1,000 eggs. The young, pencil-sized snakes have an egg tooth to help them hatch from the yellowish-white leathery eggs. Mothers tend to hang around for a few days after the hatching but then leave the youngsters to disperse and fend for themselves. The venom of this shy and elusive snake is completely harmless to humans, which is just as well as they can bite if severely provoked. One of their defence displays involves turning upside down and pretending to be dead.

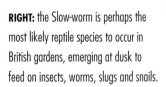

RIGHT: the Slow-worm is perhaps the most likely reptile species to occur in British gardens, emerging at dusk to feed on insects, worms, slugs and snails.

Keep a note of all sightings of any of Britain's 46 species of ladybirds and send them to the UK Ladybird Survey (www.ladybird-survey.org/default.htm), which has a series of helpful identification photos on its website. The Seven-spot Ladybird and Two-spot

Ladybird are among the most widespread and commonly seen species.

The progress of the introduced Harlequin Ladybird can be monitored at www.harlequin-survey.org, where you can also report your sightings of this species.

| Seven-spot Ladybird | Two-spot Ladybird | Twenty-two-spot Ladybird |

Invertebrates

Towards the end of autumn, many of our hibernating insects will be hidden away in a cool, dark place until the following spring. We can really help animals by supplying perfect tailor-made hibernation homes in our gardens. For more information on this, refer to Part One of this book. Supplying a home for insects can vary from the very basic bunch-of-twigs model up to the bespoke and luxurious versions available from specialist stores. To be honest, all these homes are simply trying to re-create natural nooks and crannies that might otherwise be absent in the garden.

A simple insect home which will be used by a variety of species can be made by binding together a bunch of hollow bamboo stems, then making them waterproof, either by putting them in pipes or wrapping in tarpaulin.

Ladybirds and lacewings will be on the lookout for hibernation sites. Keeping these insects in your garden over winter will help with aphid pest control in the following spring and summer.

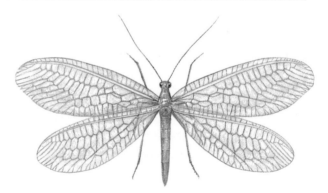

ABOVE: Green Lacewing adults and young both prey on aphids.

Bumblebees are the most important pollinators in gardens and at the moment they need all the help they can get as numbers have declined dramatically over recent years. Only the fertilized queen hibernates over winter; as well as making use of artificial homes such as a Kapok-filled earthenware flowerpot half buried with the hole exposed, she'll crawl into any frost-free nook and cranny.

ABOVE: the Garden or Orb-weaving Spider is one of the very few species in Britain capable of biting humans.

It is always a treat to watch the stunning aerial acrobatics of dragonflies as they zoom around in search of insects. There are about nine species of dragonfly likely to occur in the garden environment. The Common Darter and the Southern Hawker are two of the final species to emerge each year. They take to the wing from July and the latter continue to be seen into September while the former last into early winter, with some remaining into November if conditions permit.

Autumn sees craneflies, otherwise known as a 'daddy longlegs', emerge in force. If you see one apparently hammering itself against the lawn it will be a female pushing its eggs into the ground. There are nearly 300 species of cranefly in Britain but *Tipula paludosa* is the most common garden species. Cranefly larvae are called leatherjackets. They hatch two weeks after egg-laying and are a vital food for many birds

ABOVE: once mating is over, female craneflies deposit their eggs in the ground, where they hatch into larvae that are known as leatherjackets.

including crows and Starlings.

Autumn is a busy time for spiders as many species now mate and lay eggs. The most familiar spider is aptly named Garden Spider but is also known as the Orb-weaving or Cross Spider due to the obvious white cross on the back of its abdomen. You can often find them sitting in their huge webs; if they are not at home, try gently tapping the web with a blade of grass and with any luck an inquisitive spider will come rushing out. These spiders get bigger and bigger during the course of the year and by autumn large females are swollen with eggs. Once laid the eggs are wrapped in a silk cocoon and then guarded until the female dies in late autumn. If the cocoon survives the winter, the spiderlings will hatch in spring. The massive orb web is best seen in early morning, when beads of dew clinging to the threads emphasise its structure.

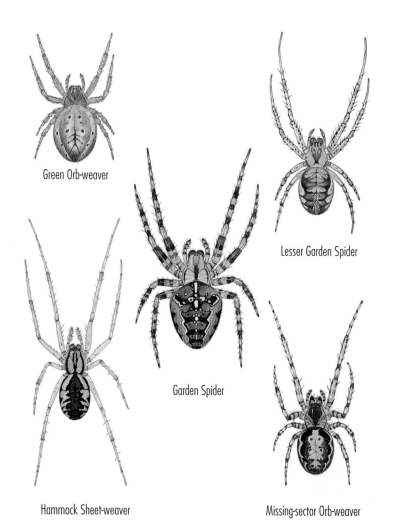

Green Orb-weaver

Lesser Garden Spider

Garden Spider

Hammock Sheet-weaver

Missing-sector Orb-weaver

ABOVE: the Common Darter is one of Britain's most common species of dragonfly and remains on the wing into October and even beyond.

APPENDIX I: Useful websites

Wildlife gardening

Beautiful Britain (www.beautifulbritain.co.uk)

Buglife (www.buglife.org.uk/getinvolved/gardening/)

English Nature: advice on wildlife gardening (www.plantpress.com/wildlife/documents.php?ct=116)

Garden Advice (www.gardenadvice.co.uk)

Garden Organic (www.gardenorganic.org.uk/factsheets/gg40.php)

Gardening for bats (www.whelan.me.uk/bats/garden4.htm)

Green Gardener (www.greengardener.co.uk)

Plants for butterflies (www.englishplants.co.uk/Bplants.html)

RSPB gardening advice (www.rspb.org.uk/advice/gardening/)

Wildlife in the Garden (www.yptenc.org.uk/docs/factsheets/ env_facts/wildlife_garden.html)

Birds

British Garden Birds (www.garden-birds.co.uk)

British Trust for Ornithology (www.bto.org)

Royal Society for the Protection of Birds (www.rspb.org.uk)

RSPB feeding advice (www.rspb.org.uk/advice/helpingbirds/feeding/index.asp)

Mammals

Bat Conservation Trust (www.bats.org.uk)

BTO – garden mammals (www.bto.org/gbw/mammals)

The Mammal Society (www.abdn.ac.uk/mammal)

The Mammal Trust (www.mtuk.org)

Royal Society for the Prevention of Cruelty to Animals (www.rspca.org.uk)

Invertebrates

British Arachnological Society (www.britishspiders.org.uk)

British Dragonfly Society (www.dragonflysoc.org.uk)

Buglife – the Invertebrate Conservation Trust (www.buglife.org.uk)

Butterfly Conservation (www.butterfly-conservation.org)

Reptiles and amphibians

British Reptiles (www.wildlifetrust.org.uk/facts/reptile.htm)

Froglife (www.froglife.org)

Reptiles and Amphibians of the UK (www.herpetofauna.co.uk)

General

Photographing garden birds (www.wildlifewatchingsupplies.co.uk/photo_tips/garden_birds.htm)

Space for Nature (www.spacefornature.co.uk)

The Wildlife Trusts (www.wildlifetrusts.org)

Wildlife cameras (www.greengardener.co.uk/wildlifebird.htm)

Woodland Trust Phenology Network (http://recording.phenology.org.uk/springwatch/)

APPENDIX II: Scientific names of species mentioned in the text

Invertebrates

Angle Shades
Phlogophora meticulosa

Azure Damselfly
Coenagrion puella

Black-and-red Froghopper
Cercopis vulnerata

Blue-tailed Damselfly
Ischnura pumilio

Brimstone
Gonepteryx rhamni

Broad-bodied Chaser
Libellula depressa

Brown-lipped Snail
Cepaea nemoralis

Buff-tailed Bumblebee
Bombus terrestris

Bumblebee hoverfly
Volucella bombylans

Cinnabar *Tyria jacobaeae*

Cockchafer
Melolontha melolontha

Comma *Polygonia c-album*

Common Blue (butterfly)
Polyommatus icarus

Common Blue Damselfly
Enallagma cyathigerum

Common Darter
Sympetrum striolatum

Common Quaker
Orthosia cerasi

Common Snail *Helix aspersa*

Common Wasp
Vespula vulgaris

Crab spider *Misumena vatia*

Cranefly *Tipula paludosa*

Cuckoo Bee
Melecta albifrons

Dark Sword-grass
Agrotis ipsilon

Dock Leaf Bug
Coreus marginatus

Dotted Bee-fly
Bombylius discolor

Early Bumblebee
Bombus pratorum

Emperor Dragonfly
Anax imperator

Garden Spider
Araneus diadematus

Gatekeeper *Pyronia tithonus*

German Wasp
Vespula germanica

Glow-worm *Lampyris noctiluca*

Green Orb-weaver
Araniella cucurbitina

Green-veined White
Pieris napi

Hammock Sheet-weaver
Linyphia triangularis

Harlequin Ladybird
Harmonia axyridis

Hebrew Character
Orthosia gothica

Holly Blue
Celastrina argiolus

Hornet *Vespa crabro*

Hoverfly spp.
Epistrophe grossulariae
Episyrphus balteatus
Eristalis tenax
Helophilus pendulus
Syrphus ribesii
Volucella pellucens
Volucella zonaria

Hummingbird Hawkmoth
Macroglossum stellatarum

Jersey Tiger
Euplagia quadripunctaria

Large Bee-fly
Bombylius major

Large Red Damselfly
Pyrrhosoma nymphula

Lesser Garden Spider
Meta segmentata

Lesser Stag Beetle
Dorcus parallelopipedus

Magpie moth
Abraxas grossulariata

Missing-sector Orb-weaver
Zygiella x-notata

Monarch Butterfly
Danaus plexippus

Orange Tip
Anthocharis cardamines

Painted Lady *Vanessa cardui*

Peacock *Inachis io*

Red Admiral
Vanessa atalanta

Rounded Snail
Discus rotundatus

Seven-spot Ladybird
Coccinella 7-punctata

Silver-Y Moth
Autographa gamma

Small Tortoiseshell
Aglais urticae

Southern Hawker
Aeshna cyanea

Speckled Wood
Pararge aegeria

Spring Flower Bee
Anthophora plumipes

Stag Beetle *Lucanus cervus*

Strawberry Snail
Trichia striolata

Thick-legged Flower-beetle
Oedemera nobilis

Two-spot Ladybird
Adalia 2-punctata

White Admiral
Limenitis camilla

White-lipped Snail
Cepaea hortensis

White-tailed Bumblebee

Bombus lucorum

Wolf spider *Pardosa sp.*

Woodlouse-eating spider
Dysdera crocota

Woolly Hoverfly
Criorhina floccosa

Birds

American Robin
Turdus migratorius

Baltimore Oriole
Icterus galbula

Black Redstart
Phoenicurus ochruros

Blackbird *Turdus merula*

Blackcap *Sylvia atricapilla*

Blue Tit *Cyanistes caeruleus*

Brambling
Fringilla montifringilla

Bullfinch *Pyrrhula pyrrhula*

Chaffinch *Fringilla coelebs*

Collared Dove
Streptopelia decaocto

Common Chiffchaff
Phylloscopus collybita

Common Redstart
Phoenicurus phoenicurus

Common Swift *Apus apus*

Common Whitethroat
Sylvia communis

Cuckoo *Cuculus canorus*

Dunnock *Prunella modularis*

European Bee-eater
Merops apiaster

Fieldfare *Turdus pilaris*

Firecrest
Regulus ignicapilla

Garden Warbler *Sylvia borin*

Goldcrest *Regulus regulus*

Goldfinch *Carduelis carduelis*

Great Spotted Woodpecker
Dendrocopos major

Great Tit *Parus major*

Greenfinch *Carduelis chloris*

House Martin
Delichon urbicum

House Sparrow
Passer domesticus

Jay *Garrulus glandarius*

Lesser Whitethroat
Sylvia curruca

Long-tailed Tit
Aegithalos caudatus

Magpie *Pica pica*

Mistle Thrush
Turdus viscivorus

Nightingale
Luscinia megarhynchos

Pied Wagtail *Motacilla alba*

Redwing *Turdus iliacus*

Reed Bunting
Emberiza schoeniclus

Robin *Erithacus rubecula*

Sand Martin *Riparia riparia*

Sedge Warbler *Acrocephalus schoenobaenus*

Siskin *Carduelis spinus*

Song Thrush
Turdus philomelos

Sparrowhawk
Accipiter nisus

Spotted Flycatcher
Muscicapa striata

Starling *Sturnus vulgaris*

Swallow *Hirundo rustica*

Tawny Owl *Strix aluco*

Treecreeper
Certhia familiaris

Turtle Dove
Streptopelia turtur

Waxwing
Bombycilla garrulus

Willow Warbler
Phylloscopus trochilus